• • •

MY FOLKS

DON'T WANT ME

TO TALK ABOUT

SLAVERY

• • •

OTHER BOOKS BY BELINDA HURMENCE

TOUGH TIFFANY

A GIRL CALLED BOY

TANCY

• • •

MY FOLKS
DON'T WANT ME
TO TALK ABOUT
SLAVERY

• • •

Twenty-one Oral Histories of
Former North Carolina Slaves
Edited by Belinda Hurmence

JOHN F. BLAIR, Publisher
Winston-Salem, North Carolina

Sixteenth Printing, 2001

Cover photograph of W. L. Bost
courtesy of The Library of Congress

Library of Congress Cataloging-in-Publication Data
Main entry under title:

My folks don't want me to talk about slavery.
Bibliography: p.
1. Slaves—North Carolina—Biography. 2. Afro-Ameri-
cans—North Carolina—Biography. 3. North Carolina—
Biography. 4. Oral history.
I. Hurmence, Belinda.
E445.N8M9 1984   975.6'00496073'00922 [B] 84-16891
ISBN 0-89587-039-8

COVER DESIGN BY DEBRA LONG HAMPTON

♦ ♦ ♦

For my parents
Eula and Warren Watson

◆　◆　◆

Contents

Introduction

SARAH DEBRO, once a slave in Orange County, North Carolina, put it bluntly: "My folks don't want me to talk about slavery. They's shame niggers ever was slaves."

Sarah's folks are not alone in their embarrassment. Many Americans, white and black, prefer to overlook Sarah's role in that period of United States history. After all, "we" aren't the ones to blame for her enslavement. Why bring it up now? Why talk about slavery?

The answer is *Sarah*. To ignore her life under slavery is to ignore black pioneering in the United States— and, in effect, to deny Sarah's humanity, as it was denied in slavery time. That is why Sarah must be allowed to speak for herself. That is why it is important to talk about slavery.

From the time the new republic came into being, Americans wrestled with the problem of Sarah. Her very existence mocked the validity of a government that guaranteed liberty and justice for the nation's people. One argument maintained that Sarah was property, not a person. The Bible was cited as proof of her inferiority. The argument prevailed, for economic reasons, and a system of government grew up around Sarah that provided for her liability under the law

ix

without providing her with protection under that same law. She could not vote; she could not marry; any children she bore became the property of her master.

The system worked well enough that millions of slaves remained in bondage for 246 years in America. It worked poorly enough that increasingly restrictive Slave Codes had to be written to keep the human property under control. Slaves must not be allowed to read and write. Slaves must not be allowed to buy and sell merchandise. There must be no guns, no riding horses without permission, no gambling, no liquor, no preaching or holding religious services or other meetings, no slandering a free white person, no insolence to a free white person—the list grew longer with each new Code. Yet the slaves persisted in behaving like human beings. They experienced the same passions as their masters: joy and sorrow, love and hatred, generosity and greed. They had dreams and hopes, and they were aware of their dreams and hopes in the way that all people are aware. The Code that governed them never succeeded in eradicating their humanity.

When freedom came to blacks in 1865, hard times came too. Some former slaves complained that their sufferings had not ended with the War Between the States. At least in the old days there had been certainty of food, clothing, shelter. Now there was no certainty, and nobody would listen to their problems.

It was true that nobody wanted to listen. The defeated, smarting South had troubles of its own, and a stunned North, the victor, suddenly had four million needy new citizens clamoring for jobs, education, some land of their own. North and South, so lately enemies, united in bewilderment. The slaves had been set free; why weren't they more grateful? Their unseemly grievances tarnished America's image. If they wouldn't put their past behind them, they ought at least, for history's sake, to keep quiet about it.

And in fact, it took little to silence them. Their children, like Sarah Debro's folks, had stopped listening to slavery stories. Besides, the ex-slaves were accustomed to going unheard, just as though they did not exist. Before long they actually would not exist, for they were growing old. Soon everybody who had experienced slavery would be dead, forever silenced.

Then, unexpectedly, in the midst of the Great Depression of the 1930s, a government agency urged them to speak up, to tell what they remembered of life under slavery. The Federal Writers' Project, created to provide work for jobless writers and researchers, initiated a program in which field workers interviewed ex-slaves wherever they might be found. More than two thousand former slaves participated in the program. Of these, 176 were North Carolinians, among them Sarah Debro.

The ex-slaves talked; the field workers wrote down what they said. Ten thousand typewritten pages of oral histories, assembled under the heading *Slave Narratives*, were deposited in the Library of Congress. There the manuscript remains intact, save for those portions claimed by individual state archives.

Several years ago, I set out to read *Slave Narratives*. Captivated by a world the history books had never told me about, I marveled at the treasure that lay in our country's library-storehouse. The people came alive in the *Narratives*, and their unique memoir gave me a fresh look at pioneering in the United States and at frontier life in my own state of North Carolina. Slaves could not legally own land as a white homesteader could, but in the sense of the self-sufficiency for which Americans admire their forebears—working the land, building houses, growing and preparing food—slaves were genuine homesteaders. They not only did the work; they endured through bondage to freedom. The idea for *My Folks Don't Want Me to Talk about Slavery* grew out of my admiration of those very real pioneers, and the book is here presented in acknowledgment of the black contribution to the nation's development, and to the development of North Carolina in particular.

Some readers may find it puzzling that the people of *My Folks* can speak of their former masters with affection, can even declare, as the ex-slave Mary Anderson does, "I think slavery was a mighty good thing for Mother, Father, me, and the other members of the family . . . ." Such a statement is almost incomprehensible to students educated after the civil rights advances of the 1960s.

The reader needs to keep in mind that these oral histories were collected half a century ago, in a time of depression and deep poverty for many whites and most blacks. The entire nation looked backward with nostalgia during the 1930s. To an aging, destitute black person, bondage may well have seemed less onerous in retrospect, particularly if coupled with memories of an easygoing master, a full stomach, the energy of childhood.

Also, some of the accounts may have been skewed, as all oral histories are likely to be to some extent, by the subjects' telling what they believed their questioners wanted to hear. And the fact that many of the interviewers were white may have constrained some of those interviewed to represent slavery as more benign than it actually was.

Nevertheless, taken as a whole, the oral histories of America's former slaves ring true. The very artlessness of the ex-slaves bestows authenticity upon their words. The same can almost be said of the interviewers, for few of that small army of field workers were skilled in the task given them. They were supplied with a list of questions to ask, told to write down the answers as nearly verbatim as possible, and by and large that is what they did. The result is a remarkably eloquent prose.

Choosing a reasonable sampling of the 176 North Carolina *Slave Narratives* at first appeared a hopeless task. Nearly every individual expressed some special viewpoint that I felt reluctant to omit. I finally made an arbitrary selection on the basis of the narrator's age, so that only histories of those slaves who were about ten years of age or older at the time freedom came are here included. Recollections of younger individuals are more likely to be based on hearsay, and the intent of the selection is to render accounts of actual experience or observation. Cutting was needed, in some instances, to eliminate hearsay, and I also made minor cuts of material either repeated or implied elsewhere in the same interview.

I have not corrected the grammar of *Slave Narratives*, since the reader will surely appreciate that errors are to be expected from unlettered persons. I did correct certain misspellings used by the interviewers to register dialect, because they seemed to me excessive and hampered readability. I also adjusted sentence order in those histories that seemed to me diffuse and rambling in organization, but this latter editing was done solely for clarity, and in no case have I altered the style of the narrators or their meaning. I am responsible for editing the *Narratives* here presented, but all the words of those narratives are the ex-slaves' own. In these pages, North Carolina's Sarah Debro and her fellow black pioneers talk about slavery, and they speak for themselves.

BELINDA HURMENCE

♦ ♦ ♦

MY FOLKS

DON'T WANT ME

TO TALK ABOUT

SLAVERY

♦ ♦ ♦

◆　◆　◆

Ann Parker

*Age 103 (?) when interviewed in
the Wake County Home, Raleigh, N.C.,
by Mary A. Hicks*

I RECKON THAT I IS a hundred and three or a hundred
and four years old. I was a woman grown at the end
of the war.

I ain't had no daddy, 'cause queens don't marry,
and my mammy, Junny, was a queen in Africa. They
kidnaps her and steals her away from her throne and
fetches her here to Wake County in slavery.

We belonged to Mr. Abner Parker, who lived near
Raleigh, and he had maybe a hundred slaves and a
whole heap of land. I ain't never liked him much,
'cause we had to work hard and we ain't got much to
eat. He ain't allowed us no fun, but we did have some,
spite of him.

We used to get by the pattyrollers and go to the
neighboring plantations, where we'd sing and talk and
maybe dance. I know once, though, that we was in a
barn on Mr. Liles's place when the pattyrollers comed.
All that could get out scatted, but the ones that got
catched got a whupping.

I got several whupping for this, that, and t'other;
but I 'spects that I needed them. Anyhow, we was

raised right; we warn't allowed to sass nobody, and we old ones still knows that we is got to be polite to you white ladies.

Daughter, did I tell you about my mammy being a queen? Yes, she was a queen, and when she told them niggers that she was, they bowed down to her. She told them not to tell it, and they don't tell, but when they is out of sight of the white folkses, they bows down to her and does what she says.

A few days before the surrender, Mammy, who am also a witch, says to them that she sees it in the coffee grounds that they am going to be free, so all of us packs up and gets out.

We got along pretty good after the war, and on till lately. After I gets too old to work, I sets on the post office steps and begs. I got a good pile of money too, but somebody done stole it, and now I's here in the County Home.

I fell and broke my arm some time ago, 'cause my right side am dead, and I tries to crawl off'n the bed. When I gets back from the hospital, they ties me in this chair to keep me from falling out, but I want to get a-loose. The nigger boy what helps me up and down ain't raised like I was; he fusses and he ain't got the manners what he ought to have.

◆　◆　◆

Bob Jones

Age 86 when interviewed August 17, 1937
at the County Home, Raleigh, N.C.,
by Mary A. Hicks

I WAS BORNED in Warren County, on the plantation belonging to Mister Bogie Rudd. My mammy was Frankie. My pappy was named Harry Jones. Him and my oldest brother, Burton, belonged to a Mister Jones there in the neighborhood.

Marster Bogie and young Marster Joe was nice as they could be, but Miss Betsy was crabbed and hard to get along with. She whupped the servants what done the housework, and she fussed so bad that she mighty nigh run all us crazy. It was her what sold my Aunt Sissy Ann, and it was her what whupped my sister Mary so bad. There warn't but six of us slaves, but them six run a race to see who can stay out of her sight.

Young Marster Joe was one of the first to go to the war, and I wanted to go with him, but I being only fourteen, they decided to send Sidney instead. I hated that, 'cause I surely wanted to go.

We never seed Marse Joe but twice after he left, the time when his daddy was buried, and when they brung his body home from the war. One day about seven or eight Yankees comed around our place looking for Reb scouts, they said, but they ain't find none, so they goes on about their business. The next day a few of our soldiers brings Marse Joe's body home from the war.

I don't remember where he was killed, but he had been dead so long that he had turned dark, and Sambo, a little nigger, says to me, "I thought, Bob, that I'd turn white when I went to heaven, but it appears to me like the white folkses am going to turn black."

We buried young Marse Joe under the trees in the family burying ground, and we niggers sung "Swing Low, Sweet Chariot," and "Nearer My God to Thee" and some others. The old missus was right nice to everybody that day, and she let the young missus take charge of all the business from that time.

We stayed on the Rudd plantation for two years after the war, then we moves to Method, where I met Edna Crowder. We courted for several months and at last I just puts my arm around her waist and I asks her to have me. She ain't got no mammy to ask, so she kisses me and tells me that she will.

During the course of our married life we had five chilluns, but only one of them lived to be named, that was Hyacinth, and he died before he was a month old.

Edna died too, six years ago, and left me to the mercies of the world. All my brothers and sisters dead, my parents dead, my chilluns dead, and my wife dead, but I has got a niece.

Till lately I been living at the Wake County Home, but my niece what lives on Person Street says that if'n I can get the pension that she can afford to let me stay to her home. I hope I does, 'cause I don't want to go back to the County Home.

Henry James Trentham

Age 92 when interviewed at
Route #2, Raleigh, N.C.,
by T. Pat Matthews

I WAS BORN on a plantation near Camden, North Carolina. I belonged to Dr. Trentham, and my missus was named Elizabeth. My father was named James Trentham, and Mother was named Lorie. I had two brothers and one sister. We all belonged to Dr. Trentham.

Marster's plantation was a awful big plantation with about four hundred slaves on it. It was a short distance from the Wateree River. Marster lived in a large two-story house with about twelve rooms in it. We called it the plantation house. Marster and Missus rode around in a carriage drawn by two horses and driven by a driver. They had four women to work in the house as cooks, maids, and the like.

The slave houses looked like a small town, and there was grist mills for corn, cotton gin, shoe shops, tanning yards, and lots of looms for weaving cloth. Most of the slaves cooked at their own houses, that they called shacks. They was give a 'lowance of rations every week. The rations was tolerably good, just about like people eat now. Our marster looked after us when we got sick.

Marster had four overseers on the place, and they drove us from sunup till sunset. Some of the women plowed barefooted most all the time, and had to carry that row and keep up with the men, and then do their cooking at night. We hated to see the sun rise in slavery time, 'cause it meant another hard day; but then we was glad to see it go down.

The cornshuckings was a great time. Marster give good liquor to everybody then. When anybody shucked a red ear, he got a extra drink of whiskey. We had big suppers then, and a good time at cornshuckings. After the shucking, at night, there would be a wrestling match to see who was best on the plantation. We got a week holiday at Christmas. Then was the time shoes was give to the slaves, and the good times generally lasted a week. At lay-by time was another big time. That was about the Fourth of July. They give a big dinner, and everybody et all the barbecue and cake they wanted.

There was a church on the plantation, and both white and black went to preaching there. There was Sunday school there, too. The preacher told us to obey our missus and marster. He told us we must be obedient to them. Yes sir, that's what he told us. They would not allow slaves no books, and I can't read and write. I did not get any learning.

No hunting was allowed a slave, if no white man was with him, and they was not allowed to carry guns.

There was a jail on the place for to put slaves in, and in the jail there was a place to put your hands in, called stocks. Slaves was put there for punishment. I seed lots of slaves whupped by the overseers. The pat-tyrollers come round ever now and then, and if you was off the plantation and had no pass, they tore you up with the lash. Some of the slaves run away. When they was caught, they was whupped and put in the stocks in the jail. Some of the slaves that run away never did come back. The overseers told us they got killed, reason they never come back.

When a slave died, there was only a few to go to the burying. They didn't have time to go, they was so busy working. The slaves was buried in plain wood boxes which was made by slave men on the plantation.

I saw slaves sold at Camden. Marster carried some slaves there and put them on the auction block and sold them. I was carried, but I was not sold. I went with the old doctor. I was his pet. They carried slaves away from the plantation in chains. They carried five or six at a time. If a nigger didn't suit him, he sold him. Missus didn't like for him to beat them so much, nohow.

I married Ella Davis thirty-one years ago in South Carolina, near Camden. We had twelve chilluns, six boys and six girls.

Slavery was pretty rough, and I am glad it is all over.

Elias Thomas

Age 84 when interviewed August 6, 1937
at 521 Cannon Avenue, Raleigh, N.C.,
by T. Pat Matthews

IT TOOK a smart nigger to know who his father was in slavery time. I don't know my father's name, but my mother was named Phillis Thomas. I was born in Chatham County on a plantation near Moncure, February, 1853. My marster was named Baxter Thomas, and Missus was named Katie. She was his wife. I can just remember my mother. I was about four or five years old when she died.

My marster's plantation was first the Thomas place. There was about two hundred acres in it, with about one hundred acres cleared land. He had six slaves on it.

When I was eight years old, he bought the Boylan place about two miles from his first home, and he moved there. There was about one thousand acres of land of it all, with about three hundred acres cleared for farming. On the Thomas place his house had six rooms; on the Boylan place the house had eight rooms. He brought in more slaves and took over all the slaves after John Boylan died.

John Boylan never married. He was a mighty hard man to get along with, and Marster Baxter Thomas was about the only one who could do anything with him when he had one of his mad spells. They were no blood relation, but Marster got possession of his property when he died. It was fixed that way.

We called the slave houses quarters. They were arranged like streets about two hundred yards on the north side of the great house.

Our food was pretty good. Our white folks used slaves, especially the children, as they did themselves about eating. We all had the same kind of food. All had plenty of clothes but only one pair of shoes a year. People went barefooted a lot then, more than they do now. We had good places to sleep, straw mattresses and chicken feather beds, and feather bolsters. A bolster reached clear across the head of the bed.

We worked from sun to sun, with one hour and a half to rest at noon or dinner time. I was so small I did not do much heavy work. I chopped corn and cotton mostly. The old slaves had patches they tended, and sold what they made and had the money it brought. Everybody eat out of the big garden, both white and black alike. Old Missus wouldn't allow us to eat rabbits, but she let us catch and eat possums. Missus didn't have any use for a rabbit.

Sometimes we caught fish with hooks in Haw River, Deep River, and the Cape Fear, and when it was a dry time and the water got low, we caught fish in seines.

My marster only had two children, both boys, Fred and John. John was about my age, and Fred was about two years older. They are both dead. My marster never had any overseers; he made boss men out of his oldest slaves.

We thought well of the poor white neighbors. We colored children took them as regular playmates. Marster's boys played with them too, and Marster gave them all the work he could. He hired both men and women of the poor white class to work on the plantation. We all worked together. We had a good time. We worked and sang together and everybody seemed happy. In harvest time, a lot of help was hired, and such laughing, working, and singing. Just a good time in general. We sang the songs "Crossing over Jordan," and "Bound for the Promised Land."

I never saw a jail for slaves, but I have seen slaves whipped. I saw Crayton Abernathy, a overseer, whip a woman in the cotton patch on Doc Smith's farm, a mile from our plantation. I also saw old man William Crump, a owner, whip a man and some children. He waited till Sunday morning to whip his slaves. He would get ready to go to church, have his horse hitched up to the buggy, and then call his slaves out and whip them before he left for church. He generally whipped about five children every Sunday morning.

We had prayer meetings on the plantation about once or twice a week. We went to the white folks' church on Sunday. We went to both the Methodist and Presbyterian. The preacher told us to obey our marsters. I remember the baptizings. They baptized in

Shattucks Creek and Haw River. I saw a lot of colored folks baptized.

No books were allowed to slaves in slavery time. I never went to school a minute in my life. I cannot read and write.

I do not remember any slaves running away from our plantation, but they ran away from old man Crump's and Richard Faucette's plantations near our plantation. Jacob Faucette ran away from Faucette and Tom Crump ran away from old man Crump. They ran away to keep from getting a whipping.

Colored folks are afraid of bears, so one of the slaves who saw Tom Crump at night told him he saw a bear in the woods where he was staying. Tom was so scared he came home next morning and took his whipping. Both came home on account of that bear business, and both were whipped.

I remember the Yankees. I will remember seeing them till I die. I will never forget it. I thought it was the last of me. The white folks had told me the Yankees would kill me or carry me off, so I thought when I saw them coming it was the last of me. I hid in the woods while they were there. They tore up some things, but they did not do much damage. They camped from Holly Springs to Avant's Ferry on Cape Fear River. William Cross's plantation was about half the distance. The camp was about thirty miles long. General Logan, who was an old man, was in charge.

I married Martha Sears when I was twenty-three

years old. I married in Raleigh. My wife died in 1912. We had fourteen children, five are living now.

When the war closed, I stayed on eight years with my marster. I then went to the N.C. State Hospital for the Insane. I stayed there twenty-eight years. That's where I learned to talk like a white man.

Mary Barbour

Age 81 when interviewed at
801 S. Bloodworth Street, Raleigh, N.C.,
by Mary A. Hicks

I RECKON that I was borned in McDowell County, because that's where my mammy, Edith, lived. She belonged to Mr. Jefferson Mitchel there, and my pappy belonged to a Mr. Jordan in Avery County, so he said.

Before the war, I don't know nothing much 'cept that we lived on a big plantation and that my mammy worked hard, but was treated pretty good. We had our little log cabin off to one side, and my mammy had sixteen chilluns. Fast as they got three years old, the marster sold them till we last four that she had with her during the war. I was the oldest of these four; then there was Henry and then the twins, Liza and Charlie.

One of the first things that I remembers was my pappy waking me up in the middle of the night, dressing me in the dark, all the time telling me to keep quiet. One of the twins hollered some, and Pappy put his hand over its mouth to keep it quiet.

After we was dressed, he went outside and peeped around for a minute, then he comed back and got us. We snook out of the house and along the woods path,

Pappy toting one of the twins and holding me by the hand and Mammy carrying the other two.

I reckons that I will always remember that walk, with the bushes slapping my legs, the wind sighing in the trees, and the hoot owls and whippoorwills hollering at each other from the big trees. I was half asleep and scared stiff, but in a little while we pass the plum thicket and there am the mules and wagon. There am the quilt in the bottom of the wagon, and on this they lays we younguns. And Pappy and Mammy gets on the board across the front and drives off down the road.

I was sleepy, but I was scared too, so as we rides along, I listens to Pappy and Mammy talk. Pappy was telling Mammy about the Yankees coming to their plantation, burning the corn cribs, the smokehouses, and destroying everything. He says right low that they done took Marster Jordan to the rip raps down nigh Norfolk, and that he stole the mules and wagon and escaped.

We was scared of the Yankees to start with, but the more we thinks about us running away from our marsters, the scareder we gets of the Rebs. Anyhow, Pappy says that we is going to join the Yankees.

We travels all night and hid in the woods all day for a long time, but after awhile we gets to Doctor Dillard's place, in Chowan County. I reckons that we stays there several days.

The Yankees has tooked this place, so we stops

over, and has a heap of fun dancing and such while we am there. The Yankees tells Pappy to head for New Bern and that he will be took care of there, so to New Bern we goes.

When we gets to New Bern, the Yankees takes the mules and wagon, they tells Pappy something, and he puts us on a long white boat named *Ocean Waves*, and to Roanoke we goes.

Later, I learns that most of the reffes [refugees] is put in James City, nigh New Bern, but there am a pretty good crowd on Roanoke.

After a few days there, the *Ocean Waves* comes back and takes all over to New Bern. My pappy was a shoemaker, so he makes Yankee boots, and we gets along pretty good.

I was raised in New Bern, and I lived there till forty years ago, when me and my husband moved to Raleigh; and though he's been dead a long time, I has lived here ever since; and even if I is eighty-one years old, I can still outwork my daughter and the rest of these young niggers.

Hannah Crasson

Age 84 when interviewed
by T. Pat Matthews

I WAS BORN on John William Walton's plantation four miles from Garner and thirteen miles from Raleigh, North Carolina, in the county of Wake. I am eighty-four years old the second day of this last gone March. I belonged to Mr. John William Walton in slavery time. My missus was named Miss Martha.

My father was named Frank Walton. My mother was named Flora Walton. Grandma was 104 years when she died. She died down at the old plantation. Our great grandmother was named Granny Flora. They stole her from Africa with a red pocket handkerchief. Old man John William got my great grandmother. The people in New England got scared of we niggers. They were afraid we would rise against them and they pushed us on down South. Lord, why didn't they let us stay where we was, they never wouldn't have been so many half-white niggers, but the old marster was to blame for that.

Our marster would not sell his slaves. He give them to his children when they married off, though. One of our master's daughters was cruel. Sometimes she would go out and rare on us, but Old Marster didn't want us whupped. The old boss man was good to us. I was talking about him the other night. He didn't whup us, and he said he didn't want nobody else to whup us. It is just like I tell you; he was never cruel to us.

Mr. Bell Allen owned slaves too. He had a-plenty of niggers. His plantation was five miles from ours. We went to church at the white folks' church. When Mr. Bell Allen seed us coming, he would say, "Yonder comes John Walton's free niggers."

The white folks did not allow us to have nothing to do with books. You better not be found trying to learn to read. Our marster was harder down on that than anything else. You better not be catched with a book. They read the Bible and told us to obey our marster, for the Bible said obey your marster.

We had a-plenty to eat, we sure did, plenty to eat. We had nice houses to live in, too. Grandma had a large room to live in, and we had one to live in. Daddy stayed at home with Mother. They worked their patches by moonlight, and worked for the white folks in the daytime. They sold what they made. Marster bought it and paid for it. He made a barrel of rice every year, my daddy did.

There was about twenty-four slaves on the place. My grandmother and mother wove our clothes. They were called homespun. They made the shoes on the plantation, too. We had a corn mill and a flour mill on the plantation. They had brandy made on the plantation, and the marster give all his slaves some for their own uses.

I swept yards, churned, fed the chickens. In the evening, I would go with my missus a-fishing. We eat collards, peas, corn bread, milk, and rice. We got biscuit and butter twice a week. I thought that the best things I ever ate was butter spread on biscuit. They gave us Christmas and other holidays. Then they, the men, would go to see their wives. Some of the men's wives belong to other marsters on other plantations. We had cornshuckings at night, and candy-pullings. Sometimes we had quiltings and dances.

One of the slaves, my aunt, she was a royal slave. She could dance all over the place with a tumbler of water on her head, without spilling it. She sure could tote herself. I always loved to see her come to church. She sure could tote herself.

I remember the day the war commenced. My marster called my father and my two uncles, Handy and Hyman, our marster called them. They had started back to the field to work in the afternoon. He said, "Come here, boys," that was our young marster, Ben Walton, says, "Come here, boys. I got something to tell you." Uncle Hyman said, "I can't. I got to go to work." He said, "Come here and set down, I got something to tell you."

The niggers went to him and set down. He told them, "There is a war commenced between the North and the South. If the North whups, you will be as free a man as I is. If the South whups, you will be a slave all your days."

Mr. Joe Walton said when he went to war that they could eat breakfast at home, go and whup the North, and be back for dinner. He went away, and it was four long years before he come back to dinner. The table was sure set a long time for him. A lot of the white folks said they wouldn't be much war, they could whup them so easy. Many of them never did come back to dinner.

I was afraid of the Yankees, because Missus had told us the Yankees were going to kill every nigger in the South. I hung to my mammy when they come through. The first band of music I ever heard play, the Yankees was playing it. They were playing a song, "I am tired of seeing the homespun dresses the Southern women wear."

I was not married till after the surrender. I did not dress the finest in the world, but I had nice clothes. My wedding dress was made of cream silk, made princess with pink and cream bows. I wore a pair of morocco store-bought shoes. My husband was dressed in a store-bought suit of clothes, the coat was made pigeon-tail. He had on a velvet vest and a white collar and tie. Somebody stole the vest after that.

Isaac Johnson

Age 82 when interviewed in
Lillington, North Carolina,
Route #1, Harnett County,
by T. Pat Matthews

I WAS TEN YEARS OLD when the Yankees come through.
I was born February 12, 1855.

I belonged to Jack Johnson. My missus' name was
Nancy. My father was Bunch Matthews; he belonged
to old man Drew Matthews, a slave owner. My mother
was named Tilla Johnson. She belonged to Jack Johnson, my marster. The plantation was near Lillington,
on the north side of the Cape Fear River, and ran down
to near the Lillington Crossroads, one mile from the
river.

I was too small to work. They had me to do little
things like feeding the chickens and minding the table
sometimes; but I was too small to work. They didn't let
children work much in them days till they were thirteen or fourteen years old. We played base, cat, rolly
hole, and a kind of baseball called 'round town. Marster would tell the children about Raw Head and Bloody
Bones and other things to scare us. He would call us to
the barn to get apples and run and hide, and we would
have a time finding him. He give the one who found

him a apple. Sometimes he didn't give the others no apple.

Jack Johnson, my marster, never had no children of his own. He had a boy with him by the name of Stephen, a nephew of his, from one of his brothers. Marster Jack had three brothers—Willis, Billy, and Matthew. I don't remember any of his sisters.

There was about four thousand acres in the plantation and about twenty-five slaves. Marster would not have an overseer. No sir, the slaves worked very much as they pleased. He whupped a slave now and then, but not much. I have seen him whup them. He had some unruly niggers. Some of them were part Indian, and mean. They all loved him, though. I never saw a slave sold. He kept his slaves together. He didn't want to get rid of any of them. No slaves run away from Marster. They didn't have any excuse to do so, because whites and colored fared alike at Marster's. Marster loved his slaves, and other white folks said he loved a nigger more than he did white folks.

Our food was fixed up fine. It was fixed by a regular cook, who didn't do anything but cook. We had gardens, a-plenty of meat, a-plenty, and more biscuit than a lot of white folks had. I can remember the biscuit.

The white folks didn't teach us to read and write. I cannot read and write, but the white folks, only about half, or less than half, could read and write then.

There were very few poor white folks who could read and write.

We went to the white folks' church at Neill's Creek, a missionary Baptist church. I remember the baptizings at the Reuben Matthews millpond. Sometimes after a big meeting, they would baptize twenty-four at one time.

Dr. John McNeill looked after us when we were sick. We used a lot of herbs and things. Drank sassafras tea and mullein tea. We also used sheep tea for measles, you knows that. You know how it was made. Called sheep pill tea. It sure would cure the measles. About all that would cure measles then. They were bad then. Worse than they is now.

We played during the Christmas holidays, and we got about two weeks Fourth of July and lay-by time, which was about the Fourth. We had great times at cornshuckings, logrollings, and cotton-pickings. We had dances. Marster allowed his slaves lots of freedom. My mother used to say he was better than other folks. Yes, she said her marster was better than other folks.

Old Marster loved his dram, and he gave it to all his slaves. It sold for ten cents a quart. He made brandy by the barrels, and at holidays all drank together and had a good time. I never saw any of them drunk. People wasn't mean when they were drinking then. It was so plentiful nobody noticed it much.

I saw Wheeler's Cavalry. They come through ahead

of the Yankees. I saw colored people in the Yankee uniforms. They were blue and had brass buttons on them. The Yankees and Wheeler's Cavalry took everything they wanted, meat, chickens, and stock.

We stayed on with Marster after the war. I've never lived out of the state. We lived in the same place until Old Marster and Missus died. Then we lived with their relations right on and here. I am now on a place their heirs own.

◆　◆　◆

Sarah Louise Augustus

Age 80 when interviewed at
1424 Lane Street, Raleigh, N.C.,
by T. Pat Matthews

I WAS BORN on a plantation near Fayetteville, North Carolina, and I belonged to J.B. Smith. His wife was named Henrietta. He owned about thirty slaves. My father was named Romeo Harden, and my mother was named Alice Smith. The little cabin where I was born is still standing.

My first days of slavery was hard. I slept on a pallet on the floor of the cabin, and just as soon as I was able to work any at all I was put to milking cows.

Mr. George Lander had the first tombstone marble yard in Fayetteville, on Hay Street on the point of Flat Iron Place. I waited on the Landers part of the time.

I can remember when there was no hospital in Fayetteville. There was a little place near the depot where there was a board shanty where they operated on people. I stood outside once and saw the doctors take a man's leg off. Dr. McDuffy was the man who took the leg off. He lived on Hay Street near the silk mill.

When one of the white folks died, they sent slaves around to the homes of their friends and neighbors

25

with a large sheet of paper with a piece of black crepe pinned to the top of it. The friends would sign or make a cross mark on it. The funerals were held at the homes, and friends and neighbors stood on the porch and in the house while the services were going on. The bodies were carried to the grave after the services in a black hearse drawn by black horses. If they did not have black horses to draw the hearse, they went off and borrowed them. The colored people washed and shrouded the dead bodies. My grandmother was one who did this. She was called Black Mammy because she wet nursed so many white children. In slavery time, she nursed all babies hatched on her marster's plantation and kept it up after the war as long as she had children.

Grandfather was named Isaac Fuller. Mrs. Mary Ann Fuller, Kate Fuller, Mr. Will Fuller, who was a lawyer in Wall Street, New York, is some of their white folks. The Fullers were born in Fayetteville.

When a slave was no good, he was put on the auction block in Fayetteville and sold. The slave block stood in the center of the street, Fayetteville Street, where Ramsey and Gillespie streets came in near Cool Springs Street. The silk mill stood just below the slave market. I saw the silkworms that made the silk and saw them gather the cocoons and spin the silk.

They hung people in the middle of Ramsey Street. They put up a gallows and hung the men exactly at twelve o'clock. I ran away from the plantation once to go with some white children to see a man hung.

The only boats I remember on the Cape Fear was the *Governor Worth*, the *Hurt*, the *Iser*, and the *North State*. Oh! Lord yes, I remember the stagecoach. As many times as I run to carry the mail to them when they come by! They blew a horn before they got there and you had to be on time 'cause they could not wait. There was a stage each way each day, one up and one down.

The Yankees came through Fayetteville wearing large blue coats with capes on them. Lots of them were mounted, and there were thousands of foot soldiers. It took them several days to get through town. The Southern soldiers retreated, and then in a few hours the Yankees covered the town. They busted into the smokehouse at Marster's, took the meat, meal, and other provisions. Grandmother pled with the Yankees, but it did no good. They took all they wanted. They said if they had to come again they would take the babies from the cradles. They told us we were all free. The Negroes begun visiting each other in the cabins and became so excited they began to shout and pray. I thought they were all crazy.

We stayed right on with Marster. He had a town house and a big house on the plantation. I went to the town house to work, but Mother and Grandmother stayed on the plantation. My mother died there, and the white folks buried her. Father stayed right on and helped run the farm until he died.

I was thirty years old when I married. I was married in my missus' graduating dress. I was married in the white folks' church, to James Henry Harris. The white folks carried me there and gave me away. Miss Mary Smith gave me away. The wedding was attended mostly by white folks.

My husband was a fireman on the Cape Fear river-boats and a white man's Negro too. My husband was finally offered a job with a shipping concern in Delaware, and we moved there. After his death I married David Augustus and immediately came back to North Carolina and my white folks, and we have been here ever since.

♦ ♦ ♦

Simuel Riddick

Age 95 when interviewed at
2205 Everette Avenue, Raleigh, N.C.,
by T. Pat Matthews

M Y NAME is Simuel Riddick. I was born the fourth day February, 1841. My owners, my white people, my old mistress wrote me a letter telling me my age. My mother was Nancy Riddick; she belonged to the Riddicks in the eastern part of the state. My father was named Elisha Riddick. My marster was named Elisha, and my mistress, Sarah Riddick. They had three daughters, Sarah, Christine, and Mary; one boy named Asbury Riddick.

I was born in Perquimans County, North Carolina, and I have lived in North Carolina all my life. We had good food, for Marster was a heavy farmer. There were about two hundred acres cleared on the plantation, and about twenty-five slaves. The great house was where Marster lived, and the quarters was where we lived. They were near the great house. I saw only one slave whupped. I had mighty fine white people, yes, mighty fine white people. They did not whup their slaves, but their son whupped my mother pretty bad, because she did not bale enough corn and turnips to feed the fattening hogs.

He was a rangtang. He loved his liquor, and he loved colored women. The old man never whupped anybody. Young Marster married in the Marmaduke family, in Gates County. He sold one man who belonged to his wife, Mary. I never saw a slave sold.

I have seen lots of pattyrollers. They were my friends. I had friends among them, because I had a young missus they run with. That's why they let me alone. I went with her to cotton-pickings at night. They came, but they didn't touch me. My young missus married Dr. Perry from the same neighborhood in Perquimans County. Bill Simpson married her sister. He was from the same place. Watson White married the other one. He was from Perquimans.

There were no half-white children on Marster's plantation, and no mixups that ever came out to be a disgrace in any way. My white folks were fine people.

I remember Marster's brother's son Tommy going off to war. Marster's brother was named Willis Riddick. He never came back.

When the war broke out, I left my marster and went to Portsmouth, Virginia. General Miles captured me and put me in uniform. I waited on him as a body servant, a private in the U.S. Army. I stayed with him until General Lee surrendered. When Lee surrendered, I stayed in Washington with General Miles at the Willard Hotel and waited on him. I stayed there a long time. I was with General Miles at Fortress Monroe and stayed with him till he was in charge of North

Carolina. He was a general, and had the 69th Irish Brigade. He also had the Bluecats and Greentorches.

I waited on him at the Abbeck House, Alexandria, Virginia, after the war. I stayed with the general a long time after the war. I didn't go with General Miles when he was ordered to the plains of the West. I stayed on the Bureau here in Raleigh. Dr. H.C. Wagel was in charge. After I left the Bureau, I worked at the N.C. State College several years, then I worked with the city at the city parks. I never left the state after coming here with General Miles.

I got a letter from my missus since I been in Raleigh. She was a fine lady. She put fine clothes on me. I was a foreman on the plantation and looked after things in general. I had charge of everything at the lots and in the fields. They trusted me.

I haven't anything to say against slavery. My old folks put my clothes on me when I was a boy. They gave me shoes and stockings and put them on me when I was a little boy. I loved them, and I can't go against them in anything. There were things I did not like about slavery on some plantations, whupping and selling parents and children from each other, but I haven't much to say. I was treated good.

Josephine Smith

Age 94 when interviewed at
1010 Mark Street, Raleigh, N.C.,
by Mary A. Hicks

I WAS BORNED in Norfolk, Virginia, and I don't know who we belonged to, but I remembers the day we was put on the block at Richmond. I was just toddling around then, but me and my mammy brought a thousand dollars. My daddy, I reckon, belonged to somebody else, and we was just sold away from him just like the cow is sold away from the bull.

A preacher by the name of Maynard bought me and Mammy and carried us to Franklinton, where we lived till his daughter married Dr. John Leach of Johnston County; then I was give to her.

All my white folkses was good to me, and I reckon that I ain't got no cause for complaint. I ain't had much clothes, and I ain't had so much to eat, and a-many a whupping, but nobody ain't never been real bad to me.

I remembers seeing a heap of slave sales, with the niggers in chains, and the speculators selling and buying them off. I also remembers seeing a drove of slaves with nothing on but a rag betwixt their legs being galloped around before the buyers. About the worst thing that ever I seed, though, was a slave woman at

Louisburg who had been sold off from her three-weeks-old baby, and was being marched to New Orleans.

She had walked till she was give out, and she was weak enough to fall in the middle of the road. She was chained with twenty or thirty other slaves, and they stopped to rest in the shade of a big oak while the speculators et their dinner. The slaves ain't having no dinner. As I pass by, this woman begs me in God's name for a drink of water, and I gives it to her. I ain't never be so sorry for nobody.

It was in the month of August, and the sun was bearing down hot when the slaves and their drivers leave the shade. They walk for a little piece, and this woman fall out. She dies there 'side of the road, and right there they buries her, cussing, they tells me, about losing money on her.

After the war, I comes to Raleigh and works for Major Russ, then I cooks a year on Hillsboro Street for somebody who I can't remember right now, then I goes to Louisburg to cook in Mr. Dedman's hotel, and hearing about Melissa, I finds that she am my sister, so I goes to Miz Mitchel's and I gets her.

A few years after the war, I marries Alex Dunson, who was a body slave for Major Fernie Green and went through all the war. Me and him lived together sixty years, I reckon, and he died the night before Thanksgiving in 1923.

Slavery wasn't so good, cause it divided families and done a heap of other things that was bad, but the work was good for everybody. It's a pity that these younguns nowadays don't know the value of work like we did. Why, when I was ten years old, I could do any kind of housework and spin and weave to boot. I hope that these chilluns will learn something in school and church. That's the only way they can learn it.

Mattie Curtis

Age 98 when interviewed at
Route #4, Raleigh, N.C.,
by Mary A. Hicks

I WAS BORN on the plantation of Mr. John Hayes in Orange County ninety-eight years ago. Several of the chilluns had been sold before the speculator come and buyed Mammy, Pappy and we three chilluns. The speculator was named Bebus, and he lived in Henderson, but he meant to sell us in the tobacco country.

We come through Raleigh, and the first thing that I remembers good was going through the paper mill on Crabtree. We traveled on to Granville County on the Granville Tobacco Path till a preacher named Whitfield buyed us. We lived near the Granville and Franklin County line, on the Granville side.

Preacher Whitfield, being a preacher, was supposed to be good, but he ain't half fed nor clothed his slaves, and he whipped them bad. I seen him whip my mammy with all the clothes off her back. He'd buck her down on a barrel and beat the blood out of her. There was some difference in his beating from the neighbors. The folks round there would whip in the back yard, but Marse Whitfield would have the barrel carried in his parlor for the beating.

35

Speaking about clothes, I went as naked as your hand till I was fourteen years old. I was naked like that when my nature come to me. Marse Whitfield ain't caring, but after that, Mammy told him that I had to have clothes.

We ain't had no sociables, but we went to church on Sunday, and they preached to us that we'd go to hell alive if we sassed our white folks.

Marse Whitfield ain't never pay for us, so finally we was sold to Miz Fanny Long in Franklin County. That woman was a devil if there ever was one. When I was little, I had picked up the fruit, fanned flies off the table with a peafowl fan and nursed the little slave chilluns. The last two or three years I had worked in the field, but at Miz Long's I worked in the tobacco factory. Yes ma'am, she had a tobacco factory where tobacco was stemmed, rolled, and packed in cases for selling. They said that she had got rich on selling chewing tobacco.

We was at Miz Long's when war was declared. Before that she had been pretty good, but she was a devil now. Her son was called to the war, and he won't go. They come and arrest him; then his mammy try to pay him out, but that ain't no good. The officers says that he was yeller, and that they was going to shoot his head off and use it for a soap gourd. The Yankees did shoot him down here at Bentonville, and Miz Long went after the body. The Confederates has got the body but they won't let her have it for love nor money.

They laugh and tell her how yeller he was, and they buried him in a ditch like a dog.

I don't know how come it, but just before the end of the war, we come to Moses Mordicia's place, right up the hill from here. He was mean too, he'd get drunk and whip niggers all day, off and on. He'd keep them tied down that long too, sometimes from sunrise till dark.

Mr. Mordicia had his yeller gals in one quarter to theirselves, and these gals belong to the Mordicia men, their friends, and the overseers. When a baby was born in that quarter, they'd send it over to the black quarter at birth. They do say that some of these gal babies got grown, and after going back to the yeller quarter, had more chilluns for her own daddy or brother. The Thompsons sprung from that set, and they say that a heap of them is halfwits for the reason that I just told you. Them yeller women was highfalutin', too; they thought they was better than the black ones. Have you ever wondered why the yeller women these days are meaner than black ones about the men? Well, that's the reason for it, their mammies raised them to think about the white men.

When the Yankees come, they come and freed us. The woods was full of Rebs what had deserted, but the Yankees killed some of them

Right after the war, northern preachers come around with a little book a-marrying slaves, and I seed one of them marry my pappy and mammy. After this, they tried to find their fourteen oldest chilluns what was sold away, but they never did find but three of them.

Some sort of corporation cut the land up, but the slaves ain't got none of it that I ever heard about. I got married before the war to Joshua Curtis. Josh ain't really care about no home, but through this land cor-poration I buyed these fifteen acres on time. I cut down the big trees that was all over these fields, and I mauled out the wood and sold it, then I plowed up the fields and planted them. Josh did help to build the house, and he worked out some.

I done a heap of work at night too, all of my sewing and such, and the piece of land near the house over there ain't never got no work except at night. I finally paid for the land. Some of my chilluns was born in the field, too. When I was to the house, we had a granny, and I blowed in a bottle to make the labor quick and easy. All of this time I had nineteen chil-luns, and Josh died, but I kept on, and the fifteen what is dead lived to be near about grown, every one of them.

I'll never forget my first bale of cotton and how I got it sold. I was some proud of that bale of cotton, and after I had it ginned, I set out with it on my steer cart for Raleigh. The white folks hated the nigger then, specially the nigger what was making something, so I dasn't ask nobody where the market was. I thought that I could find the place by myself, but I rid all day and had to take my cotton home with me that night, 'cause I can't find no place to sell it at. But that night I think it over, and the next day I go back and ask a policeman about the market. Lo and behold, child, I found it on Blount Street, and I had pass by it several times the day before.

This young generation ain't worth shucks. Fifteen years ago I hired a big buck nigger to help me shrub, and before eleven o'clock he passes out on me. You know about eleven o'clock in July it gets in a bloom. The young generation with their schools and their divorcing ain't going to get nothing out of life. It was better when folks just lived together. Their loafing gets them into trouble, and their novels makes them bad husbands and wives too.

Jacob Manson

*Age 86 when interviewed at
317 N. Haywood Street, Raleigh, N.C.,
by T. Pat Matthews*

I BELONGED to Colonel Bun Eden. His plantation was in Warren County, and he owned about fifty slaves or more. There was so many of them there he did not know all his own slaves.

Our cabins was built of poles and had stick-and-dirt chimneys, one door, and one little window at the back end of the cabin. Some of the houses had dirt floors. Our clothing was poor and homemade.

Many of the slaves went bareheaded and barefooted. Some wore rags around their heads, and some wore bonnets. We had poor food, and the young slaves was fed out of troughs. The food was put in a trough, and the little niggers gathered around and et. The chillun was looked after by the old slave women who were unable to work in the fields, while the mothers of the babies worked. The women plowed and done other work as the men did. No books or learning of any kind was allowed. No prayer meetings was allowed, but we sometimes went to the white folks' church. They told us to obey our marsters and be obedient at all times.

When bad storms come, they let us rest, but they

kept us in the fields so long sometimes that the storm caught us before we could get to the cabins. Niggers watched the weather in slavery time, and the old ones was good at prophesying the weather.

Marster lived in the great house. He did not do any work but drank a lot of whiskey, went dressed up all the time, and had niggers to wash his feet and comb his hair. He made me scratch his head when he lay down, so he could go to sleep. When he got to sleep, I would slip out. If he waked up when I started to leave, I would have to go back and scratch his head till he went to sleep again. Sometimes I had to fan the flies away from him while he slept.

Marster would not have any white overseers. He had nigger foremen. Ha! Ha! He liked some of the nigger womens too good to have any other white man playing around them. He had his sweethearts among his slave women. I ain't no man for telling false stories. I tells the truth, and that is the truth. At that time, it was a hard job to find a marster that didn't have women among his slaves. That was a general thing among the slave owners. One of the slave girls on a plantation near us went to her missus and told her about her marster forcing her to let him have something to do with her, and her missus told her, "Well, go on, you belong to him."

A lot of the slave owners had certain strong, healthy slave men to serve the slave women. Generally they give one man four women, and that man better not have nothing to do with the other women, and the women better not have nothing to do with other men.

We worked all day and some of the night, and a slave who made a week, even after doing that, was lucky if he got off without getting a beating. We got mighty bad treatment, and I just want to tell you, a nigger didn't stand as much show there as a dog did. They whipped for most any little trifle. They whipped me, so they said, just to help me get a quicker gait.

The pattyrollers come sneaking around often and whipped niggers on Marster's place. They nearly killed my uncle. They broke his collarbone when they was beating him, and Marster made them pay for it 'cause Uncle never did get over it.

One morning the dogs begun to bark, and in a few minutes the plantation was covered with Yankees. They told us we was free. They asked me where Marster's things was hid. I told them I could not give up Marster's things. They told me I had no marster, that they had fighted four years to free us and that Marster would not whip me no more. Marster sent to the fields and had all the slaves to come home. He told me to tell them not to run but to fly to the house at once. All plowhands and women come running home. The Yankees told all of them they was free.

Marster offered some of the Yankees something to eat in his house, but they would not eat cooked food, they said they wanted to cook their own food.

After the war, I farmed around, one plantation to

another. I have never owned a home of my own. When I got too old to work, I come and lived with my married daughter in Raleigh. I been here four years.

I think slavery was a mighty bad thing, though it's been no bed of roses since, but then no one could whip me no more.

◆　◆　◆

Mary Anderson

Age 86 when interviewed August 23, 1937
at 17 Poole Road, R. F. D. #2, Raleigh, N. C.,
by T. Pat Matthews.

I WAS BORN on a plantation near Franklinton, Wake County, North Carolina, May 10, 1851. I was a slave belonging to Sam Brodie, who owned the plantation. My missus' name was Evaline. My father was Alfred Brodie, and my mother was Bertha Brodie.

The plantation was very large, and there were about two hundred acres of cleared land that was farmed each year. We had good food, plenty of warm, home-made clothes, and comfortable houses. The slave houses were called the quarters, and the house where Marster lived was called the great house. Our houses had two rooms each, and Marster's house had twelve rooms. Both the slave and the white folks' buildings were located in a large grove one mile square covered with oak and hickory nut trees. Marster's house was exactly one mile from the main Louisburg Road, and there was a wide avenue leading through the plantation and grove to Marster's house. The house fronted the avenue east, and in going down the avenue from the main road you traveled directly west.

Many of the things we used were made on the

place. There was a grist mill, tannery, shoe shop, blacksmith shop, and looms for weaving cloth.

Marster had a large apple orchard in the Tar River low grounds, and up on higher ground and nearer the plantation house there was on one side of the road a large plum orchard, and on the other side was an orchard of peaches, cherries, quinces, and grapes. We picked the quinces in August and used them for preserving. Marster and Missus believed in giving the slaves plenty of fruit, especially the children.

A pond was located on the place, and in winter ice was gathered there for summer use and stored in an icehouse, which was built in the grove where the other buildings were. A large hole about ten feet deep was dug in the ground; the ice was put in that hole and covered. A large frame building was built over it. At the top of the earth, there was an entrance door and steps leading down to the bottom of the hole. Other things besides ice were stored there. There was a still on the plantation, and barrels of brandy were stored in the icehouse—also pickles, preserves, and cider.

There were about 162 slaves on the plantation, and every Sunday morning, all the children had to be bathed, dressed, and their hair combed, and carried down to Marster's for breakfast. It was a rule that all the little colored children eat at the great house every Sunday morning in order that Marster and Missus could watch them eat, so they could know which ones were sickly and have them doctored.

The slave children all carried a mussel shell in their hands to eat with. The food was put on large trays and the children all gathered around and ate, dipping up their food with their mussel shells, which they used for spoons. Those who refused to eat or those who were ailing in any way had to come back to the great house for their meals and medicine until they were well. Sunday was a great day on the plantation. Everybody got biscuits Sundays. The slave women went down to Marster's for their Sunday allowance of flour.

Marster had three children, one boy named Dallas, and two girls, Bettie and Carrie. He would not allow slave children to call his children "Marster" and "Missus" unless the slave said "Little Marster" or "Little Missus." Marster's children and the slave children played together. I went around with the baby girl, Carrie, to other plantations visiting. She taught me how to talk low and how to act in company. My association with white folks and my training while I was a slave is why I talk like white folks.

We were allowed to have prayer meetings in our homes, and we also went to the white folks' church. They would not teach any of us to read and write. Books and papers were forbidden.

Pattyrollers were not allowed on the place unless they came peacefully, and I never knew of them whipping any slaves on Marster's place. He had four white overseers, but they were not allowed to whip a slave. If there was any whipping to be done, he always said he would do it. He didn't believe in whipping, so when a slave got so bad he could not manage him, he sold him. Slaves were carried off on two-horse wagons to be sold. I have seen several loads leave. They were the unruly ones. Sometimes he would bring back slaves; once he brought back two boys and three girls from the slave market.

The war was begun, and there were stories of fights and freedom. The news went from plantation to plantation, and while the slaves acted natural and some even more polite than usual, they prayed for freedom.

Then one day I heard something that sounded like thunder, and Missus and Marster began to walk around and act queer. The grown slaves were whispering to each other. Sometimes they gathered in little gangs in the grove. Next day I heard it again, boom, boom, boom. I went and asked Missus, "Is it going to rain?" She said, "Mary, go to the icehouse and bring me some pickles and preserves." I went and got them. She ate a little and gave me some. Then she said, "You run along and play." In a day or two, everybody on the plantation seemed to be disturbed, and Marster and Missus were crying. Marster ordered all the slaves to come to the great house at nine o'clock. Nobody was working, and slaves were walking over the grove in every direction.

At nine o'clock, all the slaves gathered at the great house, and Marster and Missus come out on the porch and stood side by side. You could hear a pin drop, everything was so quiet. Then Marster said, "Good morning," and Missus said, "Good morning, children." They were both crying. Then Marster said, "Men, women, and children, you are free. You are no longer my slaves. The Yankees will soon be here."

Marster and Missus then went into the house, got two large armchairs, put them on the porch facing the avenue, and sat down side by side and remained there watching. In about an hour, there was one of the blackest clouds coming up the avenue from the main road. It was the Yankee soldiers. They finally filled the mile-long avenue reaching from Marster's house to the main Louisburg Road and spread out over the mile-square grove.

The mounted men dismounted. The footmen stacked their shining guns and began to build fires and cook. They called the slaves, saying, "You are free." Slaves were whooping and laughing and acting like they were crazy. Yankee soldiers were shaking hands with the Negroes and calling them Sam, Dinah, Sarah, and asking them questions. They busted the door to the smokehouse and got all the hams. They went to the icehouse and got several barrels of brandy, and such a time. The Negroes and Yankees were cooking and eating together. The Yankees told them to come on and join them, they were free.

Marster and Missus sat on the porch, and they were so humble no Yankee bothered anything in the great house. The slaves were awfully excited. The Yankees stayed there, cooked, eat, drank, and played music until about night. Then a bugle began to blow and you never saw such getting on horses and lining up in your life. In a few minutes they began to march, leaving the grove, which was soon as silent as a graveyard. They took Marster's horses and cattle with them and joined the main army and camped just across Cypress Creek one and one-half miles from my Marster's place on the Louisburg Road.

When they left the country, lot of the slaves went with them, and soon there were none of Marster's slaves left. They wandered around for a year from place to place, fed and working most of the time at some other slave owner's plantation and getting more homesick every day.

The second year after the surrender, our marster and missus got on their carriage and went and looked up all the Negroes they heard of who ever belonged to them. Some who went off with the Yankees were never heard of again. When Marster and Missus found any of theirs, they would say, "Well, come back home."

My father and mother, two uncles, and their families moved back. Also Lorenza Brodie, and John Brodie, and their families moved back. Several of the young men and women who once belonged to him came back. Some were so glad to get back they cried, 'cause fare had been mighty bad part of the time they were rambling around, and they were hungry. When they got back, Marster would say, "Well, you have come back

49

home, have you?" and the Negroes would say, "Yes, Marster." Most all spoke of them as Miss and Marster as they did before the surrender, and getting back home was the greatest pleasure of all.

We stayed with Marster and Missus and went to their church, the Maple Springs Baptist Church, until they died.

Bettie Brodie married a Dr. Webb from Boylan, Virginia. Carrie married a Mr. Joe Green of Franklin County. He was a big Southern planter.

Since the surrender, I married James Anderson. I had four children, one boy and three girls.

I think slavery was a mighty good thing for Mother, Father, me, and the other members of the family, and I cannot say anything but good for my old marster and missus, but I can only speak for those whose conditions I have known during slavery and since. For myself and them, I will say again, slavery was a mighty good thing.

◆　　◆　　◆

Thomas Hall

Age 81 when interviewed
September 10, 1937
at 316 Tarboro Road, Raleigh, N.C.,
by T. Pat Matthews

MY NAME is Thomas Hall and I was born in Orange County, North Carolina, on a plantation belonging to Jim Woods, whose wife, our missus, was named Polly. I am eighty-one years of age, as I was born February 14, 1856. My father, Daniel Hall, and my mother Becke Hall and me all belonged to the same man, but it was often the case that this was not true, as one man, perhaps a Johnson, would own a husband and a Smith own the wife, each slave going by the name of the slave owner's family. In such cases, the children went by the name of the family to which the mother belonged.

Getting married and having a family was a joke in the days of slavery, as the main thing in allowing any form of matrimony among the slaves was to raise more slaves in the same sense and for the same purpose as stock raisers raise horses and mules, that is, for work. A woman who could produce fast was in great demand and would bring a good price on the auction block in

Richmond, Virginia; Charleston, South Carolina; and other places.

The food in many cases that was given the slaves was not given them for their pleasure or by a cheerful giver, but for the simple and practical reason that children would not grow into a large healthy slave unless they were well fed and clothed, and given good warm places in which to live.

Conditions and rules were bad and the punishments were severe and barbarous. Some marsters acted like savages. In some instances slaves were burned at the stake. Families were torn apart by selling. Mothers were sold from their children. Children were sold from their mothers, and the father was not considered in any way as a family part. These conditions were here before the Civil War, and the conditions in a changed sense have been here ever since. The whites have always held the slaves in part slavery and are still practicing the same things on them in a different manner. Whites lynch, burn, and persecute the Negro race in America yet, and there is little they are doing to help them in any way.

Lincoln got the praise for freeing us, but did he do it? He give us freedom without giving us any chance to live to ourselves, and we still had to depend on the Southern white man for work, food, and clothing, and he held us, through our necessity and want, in a state of servitude but little better than slavery. Lincoln done but little for the Negro race, and from living stand-point, nothing. White folks are not going to do nothing for Negroes except keep them down.

Harriet Beecher Stowe, the writer of *Uncle Tom's Cabin*, did that for her own good. She had her own interests at heart, and I don't like her, Lincoln, or none of the crowd. The Yankees helped free us, so they say, but they let us be put back in slavery again.

When I think of slavery, it makes me mad. I do not believe in giving you my story, because with all the promises that have been made, the Negro is still in a bad way in the United States, no matter in what part he lives, it's all the same. Now you may be all right; there are a few white men who are, but the pressure is such from your white friends that you will be compelled to talk against us and give us the cold shoulder when you are around them, even if your heart is right towards us.

You are going around to get a story of slavery conditions and the persecutions of Negroes before the Civil War and the economic conditions concerning them since that war. You should have known before this late date all about that. Are you going to help us? No! You are only helping yourself. You say that my story may be put into a book, that you are from the Federal Writers' Project. Well, the Negro will not get anything out of it, no matter where you are from. Harriet Beecher Stowe wrote *Uncle Tom's Cabin*. I didn't like her book, and I hate her. No matter where you are from, I don't want you to write my story, because the white folks have been and are now and always will be against the Negro.

Sarah Debro

Age 90 when interviewed
July 24, 1937 at Durham, N.C.,
by Travis Jordan

I WAS BORN in Orange County way back some time in the fifties. Miz Polly White Cain and Marse Dr. Cain was my white folks. Marse Cain's plantation joined Mr. Paul Cameron's land. Marse Cain owned so many niggers that he didn't know his own slaves when he met them in the road. Sometimes he would stop them and say: "Whose niggers are you?" They'd say, "We's Marse Cain's niggers." Then he would say, "I's Marse Cain," and drive on.

Marse Cain was good to his niggers. He didn't whip them like some owners did, but if they done mean, he sold them. They knew this so they minded him. One day Grandpappy sassed Miss Polly White, and she told him that if he didn't behave hisself that she would put him in her pocket. Grandpappy was a big man, and I ask him how Miss Polly could do that. He said she meant that she would sell him, then put the money in her pocket. He never did sass Miss Polly no more.

I was kept at the big house to wait on Miss Polly, to tote her basket of keys and such as that. Whenever she seed a child down in the quarters that she wanted to raise by hand, she took them up to the big house and trained them. I was to be a housemaid. The day she took me, my mammy cried, 'cause she knew I would never be allowed to live at the cabin with her no more. Miss Polly was big and fat and she made us niggers mind, and we had to keep clean. My dresses and aprons was starched stiff. I had a clean apron every day. We had white sheets on the beds, and we niggers had plenty to eat too, even ham. When Miss Polly went to ride, she took me in the carriage with her. The driver set way up high, and me and Miss Polly set way down low. They was two hosses with shiny harness. I toted Miss Polly's bag and bundles, and if she dropped her hand-kerchief, I picked it up. I loved Miss Polly and loved staying at the big house.

I was about waist high when the soldiers mustered. I went with Miss Polly down to the mustering field where they was marching. I can see they feets now, when they flung them up and down, saying hep, hep. When they was all ready to go and fight, the women folks fixed a big dinner. Aunt Charity and Pete cooked two or three days for Miss Polly. The table was piled with chicken, ham, shoat, barbecue, young lamb, and all sorts of pies, cakes, and things, but nobody eat nothing much. Miss Polly and the ladies got to crying. The vittles got cold. I was so sad that I got over in the corner and cried too. The men folks all had on they new soldier clothes, and they didn't eat nothing neither. Young Marse Jim went up and put his arm around Miss Polly, his mammy, but that made her cry harder. Marse Jim was a cavalry. He rode a big hoss, and my Uncle Dave went with him to the field as his body-guard. He had a hoss too, so if Marse Jim's hoss got shot, there would be another one for him to ride. Miss Polly had another son, but he was too drunk to hold a gun. He stayed drunk.

The first cannon I heard scared me near about to death. We could hear them going boom, boom. I thought it was thunder, then Miss Polly say, "Listen, Sarah, hear them cannons? They's killing our mens." Then she begun to cry.

I run in the kitchen where Aunt Charity was cooking and told her Miss Polly was crying. She said, "She ain't crying 'cause the Yankees killing the mens; she's doing all that crying 'cause she scared we's going to be set free." Then I got mad and told her Miss Polly wasn't like that.

I remember when Wheeler's Cavalry come through. They was 'federates, but they was mean as the Yankees. They stole everything they could find and killed a pile of niggers. They come around checking. They ask the niggers if they wanted to be free. If they say yes, then they shot them down, but if they say no, they let them alone. They took three of my uncles out in the woods and shot they faces off.

I remember the first time the Yankees come. They come galloping down the road, jumping over the palings, trompling down the rose bushes and messing up the flower beds. They stomped all over the house, in the kitchen, pantries, smokehouse, and everywhere, but they didn't find much, 'cause near about everything done been hid. I was setting on the steps when a big Yankee come up. He had on a cap, and his eyes was mean.

"Where did they hide the gold and silver, nigger?" he yelled at me.

I was scared, and my hands was ashy, but I told him I didn't know nothing about nothing; that if anybody done hid things, they hid it while I was asleep.

"Go ask that old white-headed devil," he said to me.

I got mad then, 'cause he was talking about Miss Polly, so I didn't say nothing, I just set. Then he pushed me off the step and say if I didn't dance, he going shoot my toes off. Scared as I was, I sure done some shuffling. Then he give me five dollars and told me to go buy jimcracks, but that piece of paper won't no good. 'Twasn't nothing but a shinplaster, like all that war money, you couldn't spend it.

That Yankee kept calling Miss Polly a white-headed devil and said she done ramshacked till they wasn't nothing left, but he made his mens tote off meat, flour, pigs, and chickens. After that, Miss Polly got mighty stingy with the vittles and we didn't have no more ham.

When the war was over, the Yankees was all around the place, telling the niggers what to do. They told them they was free, that they didn't have to slave for the white folks no more. My folks all left Marse Cain and went to live in houses that the Yankees built. They was like poor white folks' houses, little shacks made out of sticks and mud, with stick-and-mud chimneys. They wasn't like Marse Cain's cabins, planked up and warm, they was full of cracks, and they wasn't no lamps and oil. All the light come from the lightwood knots burning in the fireplace.

One day my mammy come to the big house after me. I didn't want to go, I wanted to stay with Miss Polly. I begun to cry, and Mammy caught hold of me. I grabbed Miss Polly and held so tight that I tore her skirt binding loose, and her skirt fell down about her feets.

"Let her stay with me," Miss Polly said to Mammy.

But Mammy shook her head. "You took her away from me and didn't pay no mind to my crying, so now I's taking her back home. We's free now, Miss Polly, we ain't going to be slaves no more to nobody." She dragged me away. I can see how Miss Polly looked now. She didn't say nothing, but she looked hard at Mammy, and her face was white.

Mammy took me to the stick-and-mud house the Yankees done give her. It was smoky and dark cause they wasn't no windows. We didn't have no sheets and no towels, so when I cried and said I didn't want to live in no Yankee house, Mammy beat me and made me go to bed. I laid on the straw tick looking up through the cracks in the roof. I could see the stars, and the sky shining through the cracks looked like long blue splinters stretched across the rafters. I lay there and cried 'cause I wanted to go back to Miss Polly.

I was never hungry till we was free and the Yankees fed us. We didn't have nothing to eat except hardtack and middling meat. You could boil it all day and all night and it wouldn't cook done. I wouldn't eat it. I thought 'twas mule meat; mules that done been shot on the battlefield then dried. I still believe 'twas mule meat.

One day me and my brother was looking for acorns in the woods. We found something like a grave in the woods. I told Dave they was something buried in that mound. We got the grubbing hoe and dug. They was a box with eleven hams in that grave. Somebody done hid it from the Yankees and forgot where they buried it. We covered it back up, 'cause if we took it home in the daytime, the Yankees and niggers would take it away from us. So when night come, we slipped out and toted them hams to the house and hid them in the loft.

Them was bad days. I'd rather been a slave than to been hired out like I was, 'cause I wasn't no field hand, I was a handmaid, trained to wait on the ladies. Then too, I was hungry most of the time and had to keep fighting off them Yankee mens. Them Yankees was mean folks.

We's come a long way since them times. I's lived

near about ninety years, and I's seen and heard much. My folks don't want me to talk about slavery, they's shame niggers ever was slaves. But, while for most colored folks freedom is the best, they's still some niggers that ought to be slaves now. These niggers that's done clean forgot the Lord; those that's always cutting and fighting and going in white folks' houses at night, they ought to be slaves. They ought to have an old marse with a whip to make them come when he say come and go when he say go, till they learn to live right.

I looks back and thinks. I ain't never forgot them slavery days, and I ain't never forgot Miss Polly and my white starched aprons.

Ria Sorrell

Age 97 when interviewed
August 23, 1937
at 536 E. Edenton Street, Raleigh, N.C.,
by T. Pat Matthews

I JUST LACK three years of being one hundred years old. I belonged to Jacob Sorrell. His wife was named Elizabeth. My age was given to me by Mr. Bob Sorrell, the only one of Old Marster's chilluns that is living now. I was born on Marster's plantation near Leesville, in Wake County. That's been a long time ago. I can't get around now like I could when I was on the plantation.

Our houses was good houses, 'cause Marster seed to it they was fixed right. We had good beds and plenty of cover. The houses was called the nigger houses. They was about two hundred yards from the big house. Our houses had two rooms, and Marster's had seven rooms.

We didn't have any overseers, Marster said he didn't believe in them and he didn't want any. The oldest slaves on the place woke us up in the morning and acted as foreman. Marster hardly ever went to the field. He told Squire Holman and Sam Sorrell, two old slaves, what he wanted done, and they told us and we done

it. I worked at the house as nurse and housegirl most
of the time.

Mother and Father worked in the field. Mother
was named Judy, and Father was named Sam. You sees,
Father was a slave foreman. Marster bought Squire
Holman from the Holmans and let him keep his name.
That's why he was called that.

We worked from sunup till sunset with a rest spell
at twelve o'clock of two hours. He give us holidays to
rest in. That was Christmas, a week off then, then a
day every month, and all Sundays. He said he was a
Christian and he believed in giving us a chance. He
give us patches and all they made on it. He give slaves
days off to work their patches.

We had prayer meeting any time, and we went to
the white folks' church. There was no whiskey on the
place, no, no, honey, no whiskey. Now at cornshuckings, they had a big supper and all et all they wanted.
I'll tell you Jake Sorrell was all right. We didn't have
any dances no time. Some nights Marster would come
to our cabins, call us all into one of them, and pray
with us. He stood up in the floor and told us all to be
good and pray.

There was about twenty-five slaves on the place,
and Marster just wouldn't sell a slave. When he whupped
one, he didn't whup much; he was a good man. He
seemed to be sorry every time he had to whup any of
the slaves. His wife was a pure devil, she just joyed
whupping Negroes. She was tall and spare-made with

black hair and eyes. Over both her eyes was a bulge place in her forehead. Her eyes set way back in her head. Her jaws were large like a man's, and her chin stuck up. Her mouth was large, and her lips thin and seemed to be closed like she had something in her mouth most all the time.

When Marster come to town, she raised old scratch with the slaves. She whupped all she could while Marster was gone. She tried to boss Marster, but he wouldn't allow that. He kept her from whupping many a slave. She just wouldn't feed a slave, and when she had her way, our food was bad. She said underleaves of collards was good enough for slaves. Marster took feeding in his hands and fed us plenty at times. He said people couldn't work without eating. Many was the meals he give us unbeknown to his wife. Sometimes he brought hog haslets and good things to the nigger house and told us to cook it. When it was done, he come and et all he wanted, got up and said, "I'm going now," and you didn't see him no more till next day.

There was one thing they wouldn't allow, that was books and papers. I can't read and write.

I heard talk of Abraham Lincoln coming through when talk of the war come about. They met, him and Jeff Davis, in South Carolina. Lincoln said, "Jeff Davis, let them niggers go free." Jeff Davis told him, "You can't make us give up our property." Then the war started.

Yes, I remembers the Yankees. The Southern, our folks, was in front. They come along a road right by our house. Our folks was going on and the Yankees right behind. You could hear them shooting. They called it skirmishing. It was raining, and our folks was going through the mud and slush. They had wagons and some would say, "Drive up, God damn it, drive up, the damn Yankees right behind us." They had turkeys and chickens on the wagons and on their horses. They got things out of the houses and took the stock. They searched the houses and took the quilts and sheets and things.

The Yankees was soon there, and they done the same thing. That was a time. They took all they could find, and there wasn't much left when all got through. The Yankees poured out molasses and stomped down things they could not carry off. I was afraid of the Yankees. They come up and said, "Hain't you got some money round here?" I told them I knowed nothing about money. They called me "auntie" and said, "Auntie, tell us where the money is, you knows." I says, "They don't let me see everything around here, no, that they don't."

When they told us we was free, we stayed right on with Marster. We got crackers and meat from the Yankees, and when the crop was housed in the fall, Marster gave us part of all we made. We come to Raleigh on a old steer cart to get our crackers and meat—that was our allowance. We stayed at Marster's till Father died. I married there.

Marster died of consumption. I saw him die. I saw

him when the breath went out of him. The last word he said was, "Lord, do your will, not mine." Then he breathed twice and was no more. I sure believes Mar- ster went to Heaven, but Missus, well, I don't know. Don't know about her, she was so bad. She would hide her baby's cap and tell me to find it. If I couldn't find it, she whupped me. She would call Marster, and I doing the best I could to please her, and say, "Come here, Jacob, and whup this nigger," but Marster paid no attention to her. He took our part.

We finally moved to the Page place, about eleven miles north of Raleigh. We been farming with the white folks ever since, till we got so we couldn't work.

I married Buck Sorrell since the surrender. We had four boys and two girls, six children in all. They are all dead, except one, her name is Bettie. She works at Dr. Rogers's.

Missus died since the surrender. When she got sick she sent for me to go and wait on her. I just couldn't refuse Missus when she sent for me, even if she had treated me bad. I went and cleaned her like a baby, waited on her till the evening she died, that night. I went off that evening late to spend the night, and next morning when I got there, she was dead.

A lot of the niggers in slavery time worked so hard, they said they hated to see the sun rise in the morning. Slavery was a bad thing, 'cause some white folks didn't treat their niggers right.

Betty Cofer

Age 81 when interviewed at
the Beverly Jones homestead in Wachovia,
by Esther S. Pinnix

I CAN'T GET around much, because my feet and legs bother me, but I got good eyes and good ears and all my own teeth. I ain't never had a bad tooth in my head. Yes'm, I'm eighty-one, going on eighty-two. Marster done wrote my age down in his book where he kept the names of all his colored folks. Ma belonged to Dr. Jones, but Pappy belonged to Marse Israel Lash over yonder. Younguns always went with their mammies, so I belonged to the Joneses. Ma and Pappy could visit back and forth sometimes, but they never lived together until after freedom.

Marster and old Miss Julia was mighty strict, but they was good to us. Colored folks on some of the other plantations wasn't so lucky. Some of them had overseers, mean, cruel men. On one plantation the field hands had to hustle to get to the end of the row at eleven o'clock dinnertime, because when the cooks brought their dinner, they had to stop just where they was and eat, and the sun was mighty hot out in those fields. They only had ashcakes, without salt, and molasses for their dinner, but we had beans and grits and salt and sometimes meat.

I was lucky. Miss Ella was a little girl when I was borned, and she claimed me. We played together and grew up together. I waited on her and most times slept on the floor in her room. Ma was cook, and when I done got big enough, I helped to set the table in the big dining room. Then I'd put on a clean white apron and carry in the victuals and stand behind Miss Ella's chair. She'd fix me a piece of something from her plate and hand it back over her shoulder to me. I'd take it and run outside to eat it. Then I'd wipe my mouth and go back to stand behind Miss Ella again and maybe get another snack.

Yes'm, there was a crowd of hands on the plantation. I mind them all, and I can call most of their names. There was always two washwomen, a cook, some hands to help her, two sewing women, a house-girl, and some who did all the weaving and spinning. The men worked in the fields and yard. One was stable boss and looked after all the horses and mules. We raised our own flax and cotton and wool, spun the thread, wove the cloth, made all the clothes. Yes'm, we made the men's shirts and pants and coats. One woman knitted all the stockings for the white folks and colored folks too. I mind she had one finger all twisted and stiff from holding her knitting needles. We wove the cotton and linen for sheets and pillow slips and table covers. We wove the wool blankets too. I use to wait on the girl who did the weaving. When she took the cloth off the loom, she done give me the "thrums." I tied them all together with teensy little knots and got me some scraps from the sewing room, and I made me some quilt tops. Some of them was real pretty, too!

All our spinning wheels and flax wheels and looms was handmade by a wheelwright, Marse Noah Westmoreland. He lived over yonder. Those old wheels are still in the family. I got one of the flax wheels. Miss Ella done give it to me for a present. Leather was tanned and shoes was made on the place. Course, the hands mostly went barefoot in warm weather, white chillun too. We had our own mill to grind the wheat and corn, and we raised all our meat. We made our own candles from tallow and beeswax. I 'spect some of the old candle molds are over to the house now. We wove our own candlewicks too. I never saw a match till I was a grown woman. We made our fire with flint and punk. Yes'm, I was trained to cook and clean and sew. I learned to make men's pants and coats. First coat I made, Miss Julia told me to rip the collar off, and by the time I picked out all the teensy stitches and sewed it together again, I could set a collar right!

Miss Julia cut out all the clothes herself for men and women too. I 'spect her big shears and patterns and old cutting table are over at the house now. Miss Julia cut out all the clothes, and then the colored girls sewed them up, but she looked them all over, and they better be sewed right!

Miss Julia bossed the whole plantation. She looked after the sick folks and sent the doctor to dose them, and she carried the keys to the storerooms and pantries.

Yes'm, I'm some educated. Ma showed me my "a-b-abs" and my numbers, and when I was fifteen, I went to school in the log church built by the Moravians. They give it to the colored folks to use for their own school and church. Our teacher was a white man, Marse Fulk. He had one eye, done lost the other in the war. We didn't have no colored teachers then. They wasn't educated. We attended school four months a year. I went through the fifth reader, the *North Carolina Reader*. I can figger a little and read some, but I can't write much, 'cause my fingers are all stiffened up. Miss Julia use to read the Bible to us and tell us right and wrong, and Ma showed me all she could and so did the other colored folks.

No'm, I don't know much about spells and charms. Course most of the old folks believed in them. One colored man use to make charms, little bags filled with queer things. He called them jacks, and sold them to the colored folks and some white folks too.

Yes'm, I saw some slaves sold away from the plantation, four men and two women, both of them with little babies. The traders got them. Sold them down to Mobile, Alabama. One was my pappy's sister. We never heard from her again. I saw a likely young feller sold for fifteen hundred dollars. That was my Uncle Ike.

Marse Jonathan Spease bought him and kept him the rest of his life.

Yes'm, we saw Yankee soldiers. They come marching by and stopped at the house. I wasn't scared, 'cause they was all talking and laughing and friendly, but they sure was hungry. They dumped the wet clothes out of the big washpot in the yard and filled it with water. Then they broke into the smokehouse and got a lot of hams and boiled them in the pot and ate them right there in the yard. The women cooked up a lot of corn pone for them and coffee too. Marster had a barrel of liquor put by, and the Yankees knocked the head in and filled their canteens. There wasn't ary drop left.

When we heard the soldiers coming, our boys turned the horses loose in the woods. The Yankees said they had to have them and would burn the house down if we didn't get them. So our boys whistled up the horses and the soldiers carried them all off. They carried off old Jenny-mule too, but let little Jack-mule go. When the soldiers was gone, the stable boss said, "If old Jenny-mule once gets loose, nobody on earth can catch her unless she wants. She'll be back!" Sure enough, in a couple of days, she come home by herself, and we worked the farm just with her and little Jack.

Some of the colored folks followed the Yankees away. Five or six of our boys went. Two of them traveled as far as Yadkinville but come back. The rest of them kept going and we never heard tell of them again.

Yes'm, when we was freed, Pappy come to get Ma

and me. We stayed around here. Where could we go? These was our folks, and I couldn't go far away from Miss Ella. We moved out near Rural Hall and Pappy farmed, but I worked at the homeplace a lot.

When I was about twenty-four, Marse R.J. Reynolds come from Virginia and set up a tobacco factory. He fetched some hands with him. One was a likely young feller, named Cofer, from Patrick County, Virginia. I liked him, and we got married and moved back here to my folks. We started to buy our little place and raise a family. I done had four chillun, but two's dead. I got grandchillun and great-grandchillun close by. This is home to us. When we talk about the old homeplace, we just say "the house" cause there's only one house to us. The rest of the family was all fine folks and good to me, but I loved Miss Ella better'n anyone or anything else in the world. She was the best friend I ever had. If I ever wanted for anything, I just asked her and she give it to me or got it for me somehow. Once, when Cofer was in his last sickness, his sister come from East Liverpool, Ohio, to see him. I went to Miss Ella to borrow a little money. She didn't have no change, but she just took a ten-dollar bill from her purse and says, "Here you are, Betty, use what you need and bring me what's left."

I always did what I could for her too and stood by her—but one time. That was when we was little girls going together to fetch the mail. It was hot and dusty, and we stopped to cool off and wade in the branch. We heard a horse trotting and looked up and there was Marster switching his riding whip and looking at us. "Git for home, you two, and I'll tend to you," he says, and we got! But this time I let Miss Ella go to the house alone and I sneaked around to Granny's cabin and hid. I was afraid I'd get whupped! Another time, Miss Ella went to town and told me to keep up her fire whilst she was away. I fell asleep in the hearth and the fire done burnt out so's when Miss Ella come home the room was cold. She was mad as hops. Said she never had hit me, but she sure felt like doing it then.

Yes'm, I been here a right smart while. I done lived to see three generations of my white folks come and go, and they're the finest folks on earth. There use to be a regular burying ground for the plantation hands. The colored chillun use to play there, but I always played with the white chillun. Three of the old log cabins is there yet. One of them was the boys' cabin. They've got walls a foot thick and are used for storerooms now. After freedom, we buried out around our little churches, but some of the old grounds are plowed under and turned into pasture, 'cause the colored folks didn't get no deeds to them. It won't be long before I go too, but I'm going lie near my old home and my folks.

Yes'm, I remember Marse Israel Lash, my Pappy's marster. He was a low, thick-set man, very jolly and friendly. He was real smart and good too, 'cause his colored folks all loved him. He worked in the bank, and when the Yankees come, 'stead of shutting the door against them like the others did, he bid them welcome. So the Yankees done took the bank but give it back to him for his very own, and he kept it, but there was lots of bad feeling 'cause he never give folks the money they put in the old bank.

Miss Ella died two years ago. I was sick in the hospital, but the doctor come to tell me. I couldn't go to her burying. I sure missed her. There wasn't ever no one like her. Miss Kate and young Miss Julia still live at the house with their brother, Marse Lucian, but it don't seem right with Miss Ella gone. Life seems different, somehow, though there's lots of my young white folks and my own kin living round, and they're real good to me. But Miss Ella's gone!

Patsy Mitchner

Age 84 when interviewed July 2, 1937
at 432 McKee Street, Raleigh, N.C.,
by T. Pat Matthews

M Y MARSTER lived where the bus station now is on the corner of Martin and McDowell streets, in that old house that stands near there now. I was born and bred in Raleigh and have never lived out of Wake County. I belonged to Alex Gorman, a paper man. He printed the *Spirit of the Age*, a newspaper. I reckon you can find it in the museum. I reckons they keeps all way back yonder things in there just to remember by. He had a lot of printers, both black and white. The slaves turned the wheels the most of the time, and the white mens done the printing. There was a big place dug out at each side of the machine. One man pulled it to him, and the other pulled it to him. They worked it with they hands. It was a big wheel. They didn't have no printers then like they got now.

The old printing place is standing now. It stands in front of the laundry on Dawson Street, where a lot of red wagons stands going up towards the bus station. The old building with stairsteps to go up. They set the type upstairs, and the machine was on the ground floor.

75

Marster married Gormans twice and they was both named Mary. Don't know whether they was sisters or not, but they was both Virginia women. So my missus' name was Mary Gorman.

I never seed my father in my life. My mother was named Tempe Gorman. They would not talk to me about who my father was nor where he was at. Mother would laugh sometime when I asked her about him.

Marster treated his niggers mean sometimes. He beat my mother till the scars was on her back, so I could see them.

They sold my mother, sister, and brother to old man Askew, a slave speculator, and they were shipped to the Mississippi bottoms in a boxcar. I never heard from mother any more. I never seed my brother again, but my sister come back to Charlotte. She come to see me. She married and lived there till she died.

In slavery time, the food was bad at Marster's. It was cooked one day for the next, that is, the corn bread was baked and the meat was boiled and you et it cold for breakfast. The meat was as fat as butter, and you got one ration and a hunk of corn bread for a meal. No biscuit was seen in the slave houses. No sir, that they was not. No biscuit for niggers at Marster's.

Our clothes was bad, and our sleeping places was just bunks. Our shoes had wooden bottoms on them.

I heard them talk about pattyrollers so much I was scared so I could hardly sleep at night sometimes. I was afraid they would come and catch me, but I never seed one in my life. I never seed any slaves sold, in chains, or a jail for slaves. I never seed a slave whupped. Marster took them in the back shed room to whup them.

We was not teached to read and write. You better not be caught with no paper in your hand; if you was, you got the cowhide. I dasn't to talk back to them; no matter what happened, they would get you if you talked back to them.

Old Dr. Jim McKee, who is dead and gone, looked after us when we was sick. He give us medicine and kept us clean out better than people is clean out now. Dr. John McKee at the City Hall is his son. They pays no attention to me now; guess they has forgotten me.

I do not know my age, but I was about twelve years old when Wheeler's Cavalry come through. They scared me so much I squatted like a rat. They pulled clothes off the line and stole clothes from stores and went down to the depot and changed clothes. They stole the women's drawers and filled them with things. They stole meat, corn, and other things and put them in women's drawers, throwed them across their horses' backs and went on. You know women then wore long drawers open in front. Ha! Ha! Wheeler's Cavalry tied up the legs and front of them and filled the legs and seat full of things they stole. They just grabbed everything and went on. They had a reason for leaving; the Yankees was at their heels.

Just as soon as they left, the Yankees come. You know, there was a man here by the name of Governor

77

Holden, and the flag was a red and white flag, and when the Yankees come, there was another flag run up.

I want to try to tell the truth, 'cause I was teached that way by Marster and Missus.

The flag brought peace, because the Yankees did not tear up the town. They had guards out around the houses and they marched back and forth day and night to keep everybody from robbing the houses.

The Yankees with their blue uniforms on just covered the town. They was just like ants. They played pretty music on the band, and I liked that. I was afraid of them, though, 'cause Marster and Missus said they were going to give us to them when they come. I stayed hid most of the time right after the surrender, 'cause I didn't want the Yankees to catch me.

When the others left after the surrender, I run away and went to Rev. Louis Edwards, a nigger preacher. He sent me to my aunt at Rolesville. My aunt was named Patsy Lewis. I stayed there about three weeks, when my uncle rented where Cameron Park is now and tended it that year. We all come to Raleigh, and I have lived here all my life, but the three weeks I stayed at Rolesville.

Before two years had passed after the surrender, there was two out of every three slaves who wished they was back with their marsters. The marsters' kindness to the niggers after the war is the cause of the nigger having things today. There was a lot of love between marster and slave, and there is few of us that don't love the white folks today. I have worked for white folks, washing, cooking, and working at a laundry ever since freedom come.

I married Tom Mitchner after the war. I went by the name of Patsy Gorman till I was married. Now I goes by the name of Patsy Mitchner. My husband, Tom Mitchner, was born a slave.

The people is worser now than they was in slavery time. We need pattyrollers right now. 'Twould stop some of this stealing and keep a lot of folks out of the penitentiary. We need them right now.

Slavery was better for us than things is now, in some cases. Niggers then didn't have no responsibility, just work, obey, and eat. Now they got to shuffle around and live on just what the white folks mind to give them. Slaves prayed for freedom. Then they got it and didn't know what to do with it. They was turned out with nowhere to go and nothing to live on. They had no experience in looking out for themselves, and nothing to work with, and no land.

They make me think of the crowd one time who prayed for rain, when it was dry in crop time. The rain fell in torrents and kept falling till it was about a flood. The rain frogs begin to holler and calling more rain, and it rained and rained. Then the raincrow got up in a high tree, and he holler and asked the Lord for rain. It rained till every little rack of cloud that come over brought a big shower of large drops. The fields was so wet and miry you could not go in them, and water was standing in the fields middle of every row, while the ditches in the fields looked like little rivers, they was so full of water. It begun to thunder again in the southwest, right where we call the chubhole of the sky, where so much rain comes from, and the clouds growed blacker and blacker back there.

Then one of the mens who had been praying for rain up and said, "I tell you, brothers, if it don't quit raining, everything going to be washed away." They all looked at the black rain cloud in the west with sorrowful faces as if they felt they didn't know what use they had for rain after they got it. Then one of the brothers said to the other brothers, kinder easy and shameful like, "Brothers, don't you think we overdone this thing?"

That's what many a slave thought about praying for freedom.

Slavery was a bad thing, and freedom, of the kind we got, with nothing to live on, was bad. Two snakes full of poison. One lying with his head pointing north, the other with his head pointing south. Their names was slavery and freedom. The snake called slavery lay with his head pointed south, and the snake called freedom lay with his head pointed north. Both bit the nigger, and they was both bad.

◆　◆　◆

Parker Pool

Age 91 when interviewed
by T. Pat Matthews

I WAS BORN near Garner, Wake County, North Carolina. I belonged to Aufy Pool. He was a slave owner.
His plantation was near Garner. I am ninety-one years
old. I was born August 10, that's what my grand-
mammy told me, and I ain't never forgot it.

My missus' name was Betsy. My first master—I
had two—was Master Aufy Pool. Then he give us to
his son, or his son bought us in at the sale when Master
Aufy died. After Master Aufy died, his son, Louis Pool,
was my master then, and his plantation was in Johnston County. My mother was named Violet Pool. She
died in childbirth two years after I was born. My father
was named Peter Turner. He belonged to John Turner
in Johnston County, right near Clayton.

My grandfather—I had two grandfathers, one on
my mother's side and one on my father's side. On my
mother's side, Tom Pool, on my father's side, Jerry
Beddingfield. I never seed my great-grandparents, but
my great-grandfather was named Buck. He was right
out of Africa. His wife was name Hagar. I never have
seen them, but my grandmother was their daughter.
They had three chillun here in America. My grand-

mammy and grandfather told me this. My brothers were name, oldest one, Haywood, then Lem, and Peter, and me, Parker Pool. The girls, oldest girl was Minerva Rilla.

I had good owners. My missus and master, they took just as good care of me as they could. They was good to all the hands. They give us plenty to eat, and we had plenty of clothes, such as they was, but there was no such clothes as we have now. They treated us good, I will have to say that. They are dead in their graves, but I will have to say this for them. Our houses were in the grove. We called Master's house the great house. We called our homes the houses. We had good places to sleep.

We got up at light. I had to do most of the nursing of the chillun, 'cause when chopping time come, the women had to go to work. We had plenty to eat, and we et it. Our something to eat was well fixed and cooked. We caught a lot of possums, coons, and other game, but I tell you, a coon is a lot harder to catch than a possum. We had one garden, and the colored people tended the garden, and we all et out'n it.

There was about two thousand acres in the plantation. All the farm land was fenced in with wood rails. The hogs, cows, and stock was turned out in the woods, and let go. The cows was drived home at night, that is, if they didn't come up. That is so we could milk the ones we wanted to milk.

We dug ditches to drain the land, blind ditches;

we dug them and then put poles on top, and covered them with brush and dirt. We put the brush on the poles to keep the dirt from running through. Then we plowed over the ditches.

We tanned our leather in a tan trough. We used white oak bark and red oak bark. They put copperas in it too, I think.

I knows how to raise flax. You grow it, and when it is grown, you pull it clean up out of the ground till it kinda rots. They have what they called a brake, then it was broke up in that. The bark was the flax. They had a stick called a swingle stick, made kinda like a sword. They used this to knock the sticks out of the flax. They would then put the flax on a hackle, a board with a lot of pegs in it. Then they clean and string it out till it looks like your hair. The flax when it came from the hackles was ready for the wheel, where it was spun into thread. I tell you, you couldn't break it, either.

When it was spun into thread, they put it on a reel. It turned 100 times and struck; when it struck, it was called a cut. When it come from the wheel, it was called a broach. The cuts stood for so much flax. So many cuts made a yard, but there was more to do—size it, and hank it—before it was weaved. Most of the white people had flax clothes.

We had no church on the plantation. We had prayer meeting and candy-pullings, and we would ask slaves from other plantations. My master had no public cornshuckings. His slaves shucked his corn. He had about fifty head. The slaves, they went to the white folks' church. They had a place separate from the white folks by a railing. We could look at the preacher and hear him preach too.

No, sirree, they wouldn't let us have no books. They would not let none of the chilluns tell us anything about a book. I can't read and write, not a bit. They preached to us to obey our master. Preacher John Ellington was my favorite preacher. No nigger was allowed to preach. They was allowed to pray and shout sometimes, but they better not be catched with a book. The songs that they sung then, they hardly ever sing them now. They were the good old songs. "Hark from the Tomb, the Doleful Sound."

I seed many pattyrollers during slavery. If they caught you out at night without a pass, they would whup you. We visited at night, during slavery time. The men went courting. When a man, a slave, loved a woman on another plantation, they asked their master, sometimes the master would ask the other master. If they agreed, all the slave man and woman had to do Saturday night was for him to come over and they would go to bed together. There was no marriage until after the surrender. All who wanted to keep the same woman after the surrender had to pay twenty-five cents for a marriage license, then a dollar and a half, then three dollars. If the magistrate married you, you didn't have to pay anything, unless he charged you.

84

We got the holidays, Christmas, and after lay-by time of the crops. They had big dinners then. They had big tables set in the yard, the rations was spread on them, and everybody et. We had brandy at Christmas.

We had good doctors when we got sick. I remembers Dr. James, of Clayton, coming to our house. They carried their pills and medicine then, and left it at the house for you.

I have been whupped twice, and I have seen slaves whupped. Ha! Ha! Missus whupped me. She wouldn't let nobody else whup me, neither. I remembers what it was about as if it was yesterday. She was fretted about the cook. We was skinning Irish taters. She told us to make haste; if we didn't make haste and peel the taters, she would whack us down. I laughed; she sent me to get a switch. She hit me on the legs. When we were whupped, we would say, "Oh! Pray," and they would quit. If you acted stubborn, they would whup you more.

She asked me, "Ain't you going to say, 'Oh! Pray?'"

I was mad. She was not hurting me much, and I wouldn't say nothing. After awhile, I said, "Oh! Pray," and she quit.

I had good owners, all of them. My masters never did hit me. Missus would not whup me much. She just wanted to show off sometimes.

My master had a son in the war, Walter Pool. He was a foot soldier at first. He got sick, and he come home sick on furlough. He hired a man to go in his place at first, then the man went. After awhile, the men got so scarce, he had to go again; then he got the chance to go in the cavalry. Old Master bought him a horse, and he could ride next time. He belonged to the First Georgia Regiment, Second Cavalry, General Dange's Brigade, C Company, North Carolina Volunteers.

I saw the Confederates' General Johnson come through Clayton, and the Yankees come the second day after they come through. I think I seed enough Yankees come through there to whup anything on God's earth. The Yankees camped three miles from our plantation at Mrs. Widow Sarah Saunders' across White Oak Creek on the Averysboro Road. Her son, Captain Ed Saunders, was in the Confederate Army. She was a big slave owner. She had about one hundred slaves. She was called a rich woman.

The Yankees played songs of "Walking the Streets of Baltimore," and "Walking in Maryland." They really played it. They slaughtered cows and sometimes only et the liver. I went to the camp after they left, and it was the awfulest stink I ever smelt in my life. They left them cows part of them lying where they were in the camp. They killed geese and chickens, and skinned them. Sometimes they skinned the hindquarters of a cow, cut them off, and left the rest.

When they told me I was free, I didn't notice it. I stayed on and worked just like I had been doing, right on with Missus and Master. I stayed there a year after the surrender.

86

I think some of the slaves was better off when they had owners and was in slavery than they is now. The colored people are slaves now more than they was then. I can show you wherein the nigger's got all his expenses to bear now. He gets his pay out'n the white man, and the white man don't pay him much. The nigger in the South is just as much a slave as ever. The nigger now is a better slave than when they owned him, 'cause he has his own expenses to bear. If you works a horse and don't have him to feed, you is better off than if you had to feed and care for him. That is the way that thing is now.

I think Mr. Roosevelt is a mighty nice man. He has done me a lot of good. No man can make times real good till everybody is put to work. With the land lying out there, can't be real good times. This is my illustration. My horse died last year. I ain't got no money to buy another and can't get one. You see that land lying out there; I have farmed it every year for a long time. Through part of the year, I always had vegetables and such to sell, but now my horse is dead, and I can't farm no more. I ain't got nothing to sell. I is bad out of heart. I sure hope something will be done for me.

Willis Cozart

Age 92 when interviewed
May 12, 1937, at Zebulon, N.C.,
by Mary A. Hicks

NO MA'AM, Mistress, I don't want to ride in no automobile, thank you. I's done walked these three miles from Zebulon, and walking is what has kept me going all these years.

Yes'm, I's a bachelor, and I was borned on June 11, 1845, in Person County. Mr. Starling Oakley of Person County, near Roxboro, was my master, and as long as him and Old Mistress lived, I went back to see them.

He was right good to the good niggers and kinda strict with the bad ones. Personally, he ain't never have me whupped but two or three times. You's heard about these sit-down strikes lately; well, they ain't the first ones. Once, when I was four or five years old, too little to work in the fields, my master set me and some more little chilluns to work pulling up weeds around the house. Well, I makes a speech and I tells them, "Let's don't work none"; so out we sprawls on the grass under the apple tree. After awhile, Old Master found us there, and when he finds that I was the ringleader, he gives me a little whupping.

It was a big plantation, 'round twelve hundred acres of land, I reckon, and he had about seventy or eighty slaves to work the cotton, corn, tobacco, and the wheat and vegetables. The big house was something to look at, but the slave cabins was just log huts with sand floors, and stick-and-dirt chimneys. We was allowed to have a little patch of garden stuff at the back, but no chickens nor pigs. The only way we had of making money was by picking berries and selling them. We ain't had much time to do that, 'cause we worked from sunup till sundown six days a week.

The master fed us as good as he knowed how, but it was mostly on bread, meat, and vegetables.

I remembers several slave sales where they sold the pappy or the mammy away from the chilluns, and that was a sad time. They led them up one at the time and asked them questions. And they warn't many what was chained, only the bad ones, and sometime when they was traveling it was necessary to chain a new gang.

I's seed niggers beat till the blood run, and I's seed plenty more with big scars, from whuppings, but they was the bad ones. You was whupped according to the deed you done in them days. A moderate whupping was thirty-nine or forty lashes, and a real whupping was a even hundred; most folks can't stand a real whupping.

From all this you might think that we ain't had no good times, but we had our cornshuckings, candy-pullings, and suchlike. We ain't felt like hunting much, but I did go on a few fox hunts with the master. I used to go fishing too, but I ain't been now since 1873, I reckon. We sometimes went to the neighborhood affairs, if'n we was good, but if we wasn't and didn't get a pass, the pattyrollers would sure get us. When they got through whupping a nigger, he knowed he was whupped, too.

The slave weddings in that country was sorta this way: The man asked the master for the woman, and he just told them to step over the broom, and that was the way they got married them days; the poor white folks done the same way.

After the war started, the white folks tried to keep us niggers from knowing about it, but the news got around somehow, and there was some talk of getting shut of the master's family and getting rich. The plans didn't amount to nothing, and so the Yankees come down.

I remembers mighty well when the Yankees come through our country. They stole everything they could find, and I remembers what Old Master said. He says, "Everyone that wants to work for me, get in the patch to pulling that forty acres of fodder, and all that don't, get up the road with them d——Yankees." Well, we all went away.

That winter was tough, all the niggers near about starved to death, and we ain't seed nothing of the forty acres of land and the mule what the Yankees done promise us neither. After awhile we had to go to our old masters and ask them for bread to keep us alive.

The Ku Klux Klan sprung right up out of the earth, but the Yankees put a stop to that by putting so many of them in jail. They do say that that's what the State Prison was built for.

I never believed in witches, and I ain't put much stock in haunts, but I's seed a few things during my life that I can't explain, like the thing with the red eyes that mocked me one night; but shucks, I ain't believing in them things much. I's plowed my land, tended it year after year, lived by myself and all, and I ain't got hurted yet, but I ain't never rid in a automobile yet, and I got one tooth left.

W. L. Bost

Age 87 when interviewed
September 27, 1937
at 63 Curve Street, Asheville, N.C.,
by Marjorie Jones

M Y MASSA'S NAME was Jonas Bost. He had a hotel in Newton, North Carolina. My mother and grandmother both belonged to the Bost family. My old massa had two large plantations, one about three miles from Newton and another four miles away. It took a lot of niggers to keep the work a-going on them both. The women folks had to work in the hotel and in the big house in town. Old Missus, she was a good woman. She never allowed the massa to buy or sell any slaves. There never was an overseer on the whole plantation. The oldest colored man always looked after the niggers. We niggers lived better than the niggers on the other plantations.

Lord, child, I remember when I was a little boy, about ten years, the speculators come through Newton with droves of slaves. They always stay at our place. The poor critters nearly froze to death. They always come along on the last of December, so that the niggers would be ready for sale on the first day of January.

Many the time I see four or five of them chained together. They never had enough clothes on to keep a
cat warm. The women never wore anything but a thin
dress and a petticoat and one underwear. I've seen the
ice balls hanging on to the bottom of their dresses as
they ran along, just like sheep in a pasture before they
are sheared. They never wore any shoes. Just run along
on the ground, all spewed up with ice. The speculators
always rode on horses and drove the poor niggers. When
they get cold, they make them run till they are warm
again.

The speculators stayed in the hotel and put the
niggers in the quarters just like droves of hogs. All
through the night I could hear them mourning and
praying. I didn't know the Lord would let people live
who were so cruel. The gates were always locked and
they was a guard on the outside to shoot anyone who
tried to run away. Lord, Miss, them slaves look just like
droves of turkeys running along in front of them horses.

I remember when they put them on the block to
sell them. The ones between eighteen and thirty always bring the most money. The auctioneer, he stand
off at a distance and cry them off as they stand on the
block. I can hear his voice as long as I live.

If the one they going to sell was a young Negro
man, this is what he say: "Now, gentlemen and fellow
citizens, here is a big black buck Negro. He's stout as a
mule. Good for any kind of work, and he never gives

any trouble. How much am I offered for him?" And then the sale would commence, and the nigger would be sold to the highest bidder.

If they put up a young nigger woman, the auctioneer cry out: "Here's a young nigger wench, how much am I offered for her?" The poor thing stand on the block a-shivering and a-shaking nearly froze to death. When they sold, many of the poor mothers beg the speculators to sell them with their husbands, but the speculator only take what he want. So maybe the poor thing never see her husband again.

Old Massa always see that we get plenty to eat. Of course, it was no fancy rations. Just corn bread, milk, fat meat, and molasses, but the Lord knows that was lots more than other poor niggers got. Some of them had such bad massas.

Us poor niggers never allowed to learn anything. All the reading they ever hear was when they was carried through the big Bible. The massa say that keep the slaves in they places. They was one nigger boy in Newton who was terrible smart. He learn to read and write. He take other colored children out in the fields and teach them about the Bible, but they forget it before the next Sunday.

Then the pattyrollers, they keep close watch on the poor niggers so they have no chance to do anything or go anywhere. They just like policemen, only worser. Because they never let the niggers go anywhere without a pass from his massa. If you wasn't in your proper place when the pattyrollers come, they lash you till you was black and blue. The women got fifteen lashes and the men thirty. That is for just being out without a pass. If the nigger done anything worse, he was taken to the jail and put in the whipping post. They was two holes cut for the arms stretched up in the air and a block to put your feet in, then they whip you with cowhide whip. And the clothes sure never get any of them licks.

I remember how the driver, he was the man who did most of the whipping, use to whip some of the niggers. He would tie their hands together and then put their hands down over their knees, then take a stick and stick it between they hands and knees. Then when he take hold of them and beat them, first on one side then on the other.

Plenty of the colored women have children by the white men. She know better than to not do what he say. Didn't have much of that until the men from South Carolina come up here and settle and bring slaves. Then they take them very same children what have they own blood and make slaves out of them. If the missus find out, she raise revolution. But she hardly find out. The white men not going to tell, and the nigger women were always afraid to. So they just go on hoping that thing won't be that way always.

Us niggers never have chance to go to Sunday school and church. The white folks feared for niggers to get any religion and education, but I reckon something inside just told us about God and that there was a better place hereafter. We would sneak off and have prayer meeting. Sometimes the pattyrollers catch us and beat us good, but that didn't keep us from trying. I remember one old song we use to sing when we meet down in the woods back of the barn. My mother, she sing and pray to the Lord to deliver us out of slavery. She always say she thankful she was never sold from her children, and that our massa not so mean as some of the others. But the old song, it went something like this:

Oh, Mother, let's go down,
Let's go down, let's go down, let's go down.
Oh, Mother, let's go down, down in the valley to pray.
As I went down in the valley to pray
Studying about that good old way,
Who shall wear that starry crown?
Good Lord, show me the way.

Then the other part was just like that, except it said "father" instead of "mother," and then "sister" and then "brother."

Then they sing sometimes:

We camp awhile in the wilderness,
In the wilderness, in the wilderness;
We camp awhile in the wilderness,
Where the Lord makes me happy,
And then I'm a-going home!

I don't remember much about the war. There was no fighting done in Newton. Just a skirmish or two.

Most of the people get everything just ready to run when the Yankee soldiers come through the town. This was toward the last of the war. Course the niggers knew what all the fighting was about, but they didn't dare say anything. The man who owned the slaves was too mad as it was, and if the niggers say anything, they get shot right then and there. The soldiers tell us after the war that we get food, clothes, and wages from our massas, else we leave. But they was very few that ever got anything. Our old masssa say he not going pay us anything, 'cause his money was no good, but he wouldn't pay us if it had been.

Then after the war was over, we was afraid to move. Just like terrapins or turtles after emancipation. Just stick our heads out to see how the land lay. My mammy stay with Marse Jonah for about a year after freedom, then old Solomon Hall made her an offer. Old man Hall was a good man if there ever was one. My mother went to live on the place belonging to the nephew of Solomon Hall. All of her six children went with her. Mother, she cook for the white folks, and the children make crop. When the first year was up, us children got the first money we had in our lives. My mother certainly was happy.

Then the Ku Klux Klan come along. They were terrible dangerous. They wear long gowns, touch the ground. They ride horses through the town at night, and if they find a Negro that tries to get nervy or have a little bit for himself, they lash him nearly to death and gag him and leave him to do the best he can. Sometime they put sticks in the top of the tall thing they wear and then put an extra head up there with scary eyes and great big mouth, then they stick it clear up in the air to scare the poor Negroes to death.

They had another thing they call the Donkey Devil that was just as bad. They take the skin of a donkey and get inside of it and run after the poor Negroes. Oh, Miss, them was bad times, them was bad times. I know folks think the books tell the truth, but they sure don't. Us poor niggers had to take it all.

When I was about twenty year old, I married a girl from West Virginia, but she didn't live but just about a year. I stayed down there for a year or so, and then I met Mamie. We came here and both of us went to work, we work at the same place. We bought this little piece of ground about forty-two years ago. We gave $125 for it. We had to buy the lumber to build the house a little at a time, but finally we got the house done. It's been a good home for us and the children. We have two daughters and one adopted son. Both of the girls are good cooks. One of them lives in New Jersey and cooks in a big hotel. She and her husband come to see us about once a year. The other one is in Philadelphia. They both have plenty. But the adopted boy, he was part white. We took him when he was a small and did the best we could by him. He never did like to associate with colored people. I remember one time when he was a small child, I took him to town, and the conductor made me put him in the front of the street car because he thought I was just caring for him and that he was a white boy. Well, we sent him to school until he finished. Then he joined the Navy. I ain't seen him in several years. The last letter I got from him, he say he ain't spoke to a colored girl since he has been there. This made me mad, so I took his insurance policy and cashed it. I didn't want nothing to do with him, if he deny his own color.

Very few of the Negroes ever get anywhere; they never have no education. I knew one Negro who got to be a policeman in Salisbury once, and he was a good one, too.

When my next birthday comes in December, I will be eighty-eight years old. That is, if the Lord lets me live, and I sure hope He does.

Bibliography

My primary research source for *My Folks Don't Want Me to Talk About Slavery* was the Federal Writers' Project collection, *Slave Narratives: A Folk History of Slavery in the U.S. from Interviews with Former Slaves*. The original manuscript of this collection is housed in the Rare Book and Special Collections Division of the Library of Congress. Facsimile editions of the collection are available. One edition was published by Scholarly Press of St. Clair Shores, Michigan in 1976. Another edition, entitled *The American Slave: A Composite Autobiography* and edited by George P. Rawick, was published by Greenwood Press of Westport, Connecticut in 1972. The latter edition also includes narratives from the Fisk University interviews of the 1920s as well as an original survey volume by the editor.

—B.H.

Other Narratives, Journals, and First-Person Accounts

Feelings, Tom. *To Be a Slave*. New York: Dial, 1968.

Jones, Thomas H. *The Experience of Thomas H. Jones, Who Was a Slave for Forty-Three Years*. New Bedford, N.Y.: E. Anthony & Sons, Ptrs., 1871.

Kemble, Fanny. *Journal of a Residence on a Georgian Plantation in 1838–1839*. New York: Harper & Row, 1863.

Killion, Ronald, and Charles Waller, eds. *Slavery Time.* Savannah, Ga.: Beehive Press, 1973.

Olmsted, Frederick Law. *A Journey in the Seaboard Slave States.* New York: Dix & Edwards, 1856.

Sterling, Dorothy. *The Trouble They Seen.* New York: Doubleday, 1976.

Yetman, Norman R. *Voices from Slavery.* New York: Holt, Rinehart and Winston, 1970.

Works by Historians and Scholars

Basset, J.S. *Slavery in the State of North Carolina.* Baltimore: Johns Hopkins Press, 1899.

Botkin, B.A. *Lay My Burden Down.* Univ. of Chicago Press, 1945.

Escott, Paul D. *Slavery Remembered.* Chapel Hill, N.C.: Univ. of North Carolina Press, 1979.

Gara, Larry. *Liberty Line: The Legend of the Underground Railroad.* Univ. of Kentucky Press, 1961.

Hamilton, J.G. de Roulhac. *Reconstruction in North Carolina.* Raleigh, N.C.: Presses of Edwards & Broughton, 1906.

Higginbotham, A. Leon Jr. *In the Matter of Color, Race, and the American Legal Process.* Oxford Univ. Press, 1978.

Rice, C. Duncan. *The Rise and Fall of Black Slavery.* New York: Harper & Row, 1975.

Rose, Willie Lee. *A Documentary History of Slavery in North America.* Oxford Univ. Press, 1976.

Scott, John Anthony. *Hard Trials on My Way.* New York: Knopf, 1974.

Siebert, Wilbur H. *The Underground Railroad from Slavery to Freedom*. 1898. Reprint. Arno Press, 1968.

Williamson, Joel. *After Slavery*. Chapel Hill: Univ. of North Carolina Press, 1965.

Zuber, Richard L. *North Carolina during Reconstruction*. Raleigh, N.C.: Dept. of Cultural Resources, Division of Archives and History, 1975.